When a mix of ideas and influences with no common theme or spirit, apart from one of desperation, becomes one of the most well-known bands of the 90s …

Death Threats from an Eight-Year-Old
By Mike Edwards

Editor: Brian Paone
Graphic Designer: Amy Hunter
Proofreaders: Travis West, Douglas Esper, Jared Sizemore, Kyle
Lechner, Carl Jenkins, Geoff Turner

www.ScoutMediaBooksMusic.com

www.JesusJones.com

1.

Fireworks in Brooklyn

"Yeah, yeah, yeah. Happy New Year and all that!"

Does Scrooge's reign extend to New Year's Eve? Or is it kicked into the streets in time to join the Boxing Day sales queues, by which point I become just an ordinary miserable git with no Dickensian relevance? Whichever it is, the well-intended but requisite "Happy New Year!" had me gulping champagne, embarrassed and anti-social on the sofa while my girlfriend and her family stood by the window, *oohi*ng and *aaah*ing at the fireworks exploding over Manhattan, firing the old year into space and ushering in the new with a forest of burnt cardboard, touch paper, and hospital wards filled with second-degree burns.

I was drinking champagne. I was in a glamorous city—meaning any city abroad, except Normal, Illinois, or Stuttgart—watching fireworks in the company of near and dear, but still managing to sulk. Well, it's Christmas, the holiday period, the suicide season, the death of a year, that time, that moment when your thoughts are centred on the events of the past versus the hopes for the future. For me, on this New Year, that was a contest on a par with Godzilla versus, well, some other histrionic Japanese guy in a monster suit.

So, 1996 took a colossal swing at our hero, 1997—which took it in the solar plexus, buckled, then ... the screen went blank.

A Brief History of Mine

A true Cockney by birth, if not by accent, I was born in the city of London just in time for my parents to celebrate the release of *A Hard Day's Night* by The Beatles. My first real musical memories are from the late '60s and early '70s—rainy, South London Sunday afternoons spent indoors, the headache-inducing smell of the cigars my father used to wean himself off smoking, the child-baffling conversation of my parents and their visitors, and Beatles albums. Which I hated. Luckily, watching *Top of the Pops* was an institution in our house (as well as *Dr. Who*—the episodes of which have since had their terrifying qualities evaporate in BBC vaults), and Gary Glitter, The Osmonds, and Slade gave me a new outlook on music. It was something exhilarating, even if I was too young to wear the makeup. In the case of T. Rex, it was something worth miming to with fishing rods.

When my ninth birthday arrived, top of my present list was the single, "Hell Raiser" by The Sweet. When it was played at my birthday party, on a sunny summer afternoon, I was so excited I squirmed under a chair. Clearly, I'd never be much of a dancer. I played that record—my first single—endlessly, deciding the parts sung by the guitarist, not the singer, on TV were *my* parts.

Three months later, my parents wedged me and my younger brother in-between large quantities of peanut butter and vile-tasting dehydrated meals ("At last! A use for dried skunk!") in the back of a Land Rover and headed off in convoy with our South African neighbours towards the Sahara. This was apparently the sort of thing that got arranged in the '70s if your parents went out drinking. The neighbours were returning home to South Africa, and as it was (feasibly) on their way, we would drive around the desert with them for six weeks or so and then return. In the early '90s, ravers imagined scenes like this while on ecstasy and pretended they'd forgotten about it the next day, thus sparing us a Sahara filled with desiccated corpses in Tribal Gathering T-shirts.

Not everything went as planned in the desert. It rained once (my mother said to my father, "That's not rain, it's petrol from the cans on the roof, you bloody fool"), I destroyed a Moor's fence with my first-ever driving lesson, and in a freak but nutritious culinary accident, the peanut butter containers exploded in the heat. Then we decided to travel the rest of Africa.

While it was an unparalleled experience and a fine excuse for not being at school, at 20mph, a lot of the Sahara, the Zairian jungle, and all the bits before and after vastly expands. It was a good thing, therefore, that the Land Rover was fitted with a cassette player, and we spent six months traversing Africa, singing along with The Beatles, The Rolling Stones, Janis Joplin, Simon and Garfunkel, and other less luminary stars of the '60s—a hippie musical of a mobile Swiss Family Robinson. "All you need is love," we sang as we moved through Algeria, Zaire, Rwanda, Kenya, Mozambique, and South Africa—places that would later come to believe otherwise. In fact, just two weeks after driving down the main coastal road in Mozambique, guerrillas mined and blew it up—a definite overreaction to the family's vocal abilities. But it is nice to know music really can change the world.

Somewhere on this journey, certainly between dunes in the Grand Erg Occidental, I decided I wanted to create music like this, and a new profession replaced my chosen ones of either fireman or footballer—one that didn't begin with *F*—rock star.

For eighteen months, my brother and I attended school in Johannesburg while my parents worked to save the money to get home. It was a good arrangement and legal at least. We'd return home via the same means and with the same soundtrack.

As disco broke, we drove through Africa again, taking a sharp right onto a ship bound for India, narrowly avoiding a tornado that caused an onboard epidemic of sea sickness (I can reveal that green vomit really can be projected over a distance of many, many feet in real life, fact fans), driving through the sub-continent (I can reveal that human shit also comes in green, fact fans), detouring to Nepal, and then back through Asia: Pakistan, where everybody in a car wanted to stop us and talk about their relatives in England; over the Khyber Pass into Afghanistan, where we suffered their heaviest snows in ten years, conspiring to make it an even more beautiful country; Iran, so cold the hoar frost was inches thick around the trees and where my brother fell through ice into the Caspian Sea while my parents fought off eager heroin dealers; Eastern Turkey, where the exuberant natives threw welcoming rocks at us and where, by the Mediterranean, I got to play soldier among the ruins, re-creating scenes from the tales of Greek mythology I'd read in the Sahara and discovering that my brother had an Achilles body when it came to hurling stones and thrusting branches.

We returned to London in the spring of 1976, with my greatest concern being that my hair wasn't of the right style, unaware that terrible hair was endemic then.

At a friend's house, I investigated what was happening in music, in particular if the Bay City Rollers were actually the new Beatles or whether we'd have to wait for Duran Duran and then Oasis. After three years of indoctrination, I felt The Beatles' crown rested safe. During that blistering drought-ridden summer, I was placed at Crown Woods Comprehensive School in Eltham and witnessed the antagonism between that school and Eltham Green—the school Boy George was attending at that time—an antagonism that climaxed when a crack commando from down the hill set fire to our large sun-browned playing fields. It wasn't Boy George. I know because I asked him years later.

My father couldn't find a job in London and spent the last few months of '76 working in Corsham, Wiltshire—a town once famous for being the most graffiti-ridden in England. Although what the inhabitants had so much to write about still baffles me—and we were to follow once my parents had located a house for us. Taking the train to school one frosty December morning, I picked up a discarded *Sun* newspaper and read the screaming headlines declaiming the Sex Pistols *a band who were bringing civilisation to an end by swearing on early evening TV.* Intriguing!

On January 7, 1977, I sat in my father's car (after Morocco, he always drove) looking at the Victorian edifice of my new school, Fitzmaurice Grammar, Bradford-on-Avon, Wiltshire, with "Money, Money, Money" by Abba playing on the radio. If it was to be a prophetic moment, I'm very glad they hadn't yet released "Dancing Queen."

El Mariachi de Wiltshire

Three months later, my mother became so irritated by my tuneless and illicit strumming on my father's Spanish guitar—a guitar we'd carried with us through three continents, perhaps not such a bad idea since it probably displaced more peanut butter explosive—that I was told to stop forever, lose my hands, or buy my own. Gathering together a very short life's savings (those grandparental Christmas gifts to the fore), doing a few chores at home, and a paper round that instilled a lifelong hatred of dogs in me, I took the latter option and got a cheap nylon-strung guitar from a shop in Bath that now sells cheap nylon-strung carpets.

By this time, the Sex Pistols were further down the path to world annihilation, and I was part of the plot, figuring out the monumental guitar intro to "Pretty Vacant"—like "Hell Raiser," another single I still own in its original sleeve. "Go Buddy Go" by The Stranglers was way beyond me, even if I had now discovered the frets were there for a purpose other than decoration.

My nascent enthusiasm for punk was stillborn though, and I'm not entirely sure why. Partly, I know, it was due to a personality quirk that has by and large directed my life: everyone else was doing it, and I didn't want to run with the herd. Soon, even the kids two years younger than me (horror of horrors!) were pogoing to "God Save the Queen" at the school disco and wearing their school ties outside their jumpers (See! The powers that be were right to fear). Punk had said, "Be an individual!" and everyone conformed.

After the full-blooded roar of the Sex Pistols, punk seemed to lose its musical muscle as the floodgates opened and new bands cascaded in. To me, the first Clash album was a tinny racket by comparison with *Never Mind the Bollocks*, and it took until *London's Burning* for me to rescue any credibility whatsoever for the genre. Similarly, the likes of The Adverts, Penetration, X-Ray Spex etc. gave me the impression of people who'd look at a 500cc motorbike and design a scooter as a result. That pretty much killed the mod revival for me too.

In search of that same raw guitar power, I fell back on that staple of small towns the Western world heralded *bad heavy metal*! (Or *heavy rock*, as its adherents would argue vociferously and pointlessly). Not that I fell into it wholeheartedly. I was never one for Iron Maiden or Deep Purple or Black Sabbath or Saxon or Def Leppard. No, AC/DC were more my box of plectra, and it helped that their guitar style involved "open" guitar chords, the easiest and first to learn.

Little Drummer Boy

A year later, 1978, a new boy, Simon Matthews, arrived in our school and was welcomed with unexceptional schoolboy puerility from a few of his classmates. They would refer to him by any number of derogatory names, but his response was invariably the same: "Genital!" So often was this retort used that he became known by it, first as a mild dig, then stripping it of its barb and abbreviation, resulting in a permanent nickname: Gen.

Not surprisingly, he would gloss over this in later years. Sorry, Gen.

Another guitarist, Richard Miles, was in my class, and after a tense dispute over which is the correct key to play Black Sabbath's "Paranoid," we'd decided to form a band. Hearing Gen sing along to a Deep Purple album at a party (oh, wild youth!), we decided he would be our singer. Fortunately, he didn't object.

I bought my first electric guitar. We coerced another friend to buy a bass of utterly woeful quality and then learn how to play it, utterly woefully. We were almost a band and had our first rehearsal in Richard's dad's garage in December 1979. It was a total disaster.

Bass Bashing Harris, as he had come to be known, could hardly play. My hands were numb with cold. The neighbour's fully justified complaints stopped us after about thirty deafening minutes of musical whiteout, and Gen, hearing his first-ever vocal session—sung through a guitar amp, played through a tape recorder—decided he'd rather be the drummer. That was fine by me, as we didn't have one yet, but the problem was we didn't have access to a drum kit.

It's always at this point in a band's career when members get in based on wealth rather than talent, and drummers are far more valuable than anyone with just a voice.

Already developing my maniacal, over-bearing fervour for organising the band, I seem to remember telling him dismissively that once he got a drum kit, he'd be our drummer. He went through Hell and high water to coerce already-stressed parents into helping him. We were both lucky it paid off. I was lucky I didn't get a beating.

By February, we were a band without a singer, and our first gig—a classmate's sixteenth birthday party in a local hall—was looming. Richard called in an acquaintance, Mike Palmer—a man with all the right qualifications for the job as far as we were concerned: a glamorous girlfriend, a motorbike, a disqualification for riding that motorbike before he was legally eligible to, and a reputation for being a fighter. He was also one of the funniest people I'd ever met.

No-one bothered to ask him if he could sing. Why trip up the otherwise perfect candidate?

First Love

On May 10, 1980, Gen and I played our first-ever gig together. It was every bit as bad as you'd expect, but for us, it was electrifying—a huge surge of adrenaline with a slow burn-off of pleasure. It was addictive too.

Two months before my sixteenth birthday, just before my O-level exams, I had decided my career. And it still wouldn't involve fire or balls. I stayed on to take A-levels, not really because I was interested in further education, certainly not University—that would only get in the way of the band—but because I was terrified of going out and working.

Masquerading as an A-level student, I wrote songs, soon discovering I worked best on my own, haggled with local promoters to try and get gigs—usually in vain—and rehearsed, either with the band once a week at Mike's house or just playing guitar by myself. We played a few gigs—terrible affairs with no sound system or lights and our cheap equipment constantly malfunctioning. I played one gig drunk and discovered I wasn't good enough to carry off that trick, and Richard provided occasional evidence that he wasn't either. Playing straight became the rule.

During that two-year *A*-level course, we entered a local music competition—a Battle of the Bands. It seemed like a huge event to us at the time, giving us the chance to play with decent sound systems, and on stages too! To our surprise, we won the first heat. After that, we felt we were on to something, and the resulting cockiness was, I'm sure, what propelled us to victory. Certainly, it wasn't the music or our ability that could have swung it.

Peter Gabriel, the area's resident rock star, had been roped in to present our prize. With a smile big enough to match the enormity of the lie, Richard shook his hand and said, "I've got all your albums!" We were both overawed and overwhelmed. By coincidence, Peter Gabriel's manager at the time was Gail Colson, who, a few years later, would be Jesus Jones' manager. Thank God she wasn't there then.

Gen stayed at my house that night, and we talked about how we'd famous. We could see the path to success lying clearly ahead of us. It was frustratingly slow in coming though, so we bided our time with the trail of local gigs and writing—Mike doing the words; me, the music.

We recorded demo tapes in a studio magically free of graffiti in Corsham, where the sessions were chaotic and ran on the sort of democracy where 'he who shouts loudest or most forcefully,' wins … meaning me. It helped that I was writing the music and doing the organising—arrogance and bossiness being virtues when directing five dissenting opinions. The background—my school life—came briefly to the fore as *A*-level exams approached, and for a short while, the band was put on hold.

Right after my eighteenth birthday, school was out of my life, and I would never taste lunches like that again, until I went to Romania, where a lack of dairy products, sugar, meat, salt, and fresh vegetables at least gave them an excuse.

Now for stardom! Only it was delayed again. We played to diminishing crowds, and Mike and I travelled to London to flog tapes around record company A&R departments to no avail (although one guy came to see us play a local gig, only to refuse our phone calls afterwards). Bass Bashing Harris left for garden digging college, and I got a job labouring with our new bass player, Graham.

I started in summer, getting muscles and a tan, along with a wage packet, but by winter, breaking the ice on top of the water barrel to reach inside and grab the immersed tools every morning while Graham's Alsatian puppy ate my lunch in the van, it was less fun. I stuck it out as we were still rehearsing, and I continued writing, penning the words as well.

The arrangements got a little less basic, and Richard and I sang backing vocals, mostly because my taste for the music we were playing was diminishing, and I was trying to pull us in a more modern direction, influenced by the sort of guitar playing and sounds that Andy Summers (The Police), Stuart Adamson (Big Country), and The Edge (U2) were making. Siouxsie and the Banshees, The Cure, Blondie, and The Pretenders should have been favourites of mine long before they actually were; I was late to their party. This didn't sit well with the rest of the band, but as I had become the main writer, they could do little but follow with muttered misgivings and play defiant bum notes.

By summer '83, it was too much for all of us, and at a rehearsal, I told the rest of the band I was leaving. Richard, always the one for a great quote, just had one burning question about the issue. "Are you gay?"

Soon afterwards, he joined the Navy.

Once More, With Feeling

I spent months writing more, making dozens of home recordings by playing one tape recorder through a sound mixer whilst adding another instrumental track and an earful of hiss. Somewhat sneakily, I got Gen and Mike to form a new band with me. With a singer, drummer, and my guitar in place, we needed a bass player, so I asked the local Musicians Union rep for help. His friend ran a jazz band in Bath who had a son who played bass, a guy about our age: Alan.

Al turned up to rehearsal, looking like a spitting image of Duran Duran's John Taylor. He wore leather trousers. His dyed hair was permed. He played a fretless bass—the connotations of musicianship were not lost on us—through an amp the size of a transistor radio. He was shamelessly exhibitionist, dancing around on the venue's stage where we rehearsed while the three of us sat at floor level and played, bemused. He clearly had the musical ability. All he needed was the song's key, and he'd just solo his way through the song, playing non-stop and cramming each bar chock full of notes. He was so adept he didn't even stop when we did, he just carried on until we started the next song. He was in.

The plan for this band was to succeed where the last had failed, and that meant moving to London. We would play a few gigs to get the band to gel, then relocate to where willing A&R men and readymade contracts lined the streets. Meanwhile, Mike was getting disillusioned, partly with the music and with four years lack of success.

Two weeks before our first gig, he announced he wasn't prepared to move to London; he'd stay behind and get married. Two weeks meant two rehearsals—we couldn't afford more—and that wasn't enough time to find a new singer. The thought of cancelling the gig never occurred to us, as they were so hard to come by that they were almost sacred.

As I was now writing everything and doing backing vocals in every song, an obvious solution presented itself. I grabbed my guitar, Gen counted us in, and I became a singer.

God, it was hard! The concentration required to play the guitar lines—no more AC/DC chords now—and sing too brought me into an instant sweat. It was a huge jump, and one that took me years to complete satisfactorily, but with brash self-confidence, I was certain I could do it.

The people who complained at my singing for those first few gigs, I ignored—even when Al tactfully suggested a female singer he knew. I kept ignoring them for years more.

We moved to London in January 1985, into a flat in Walthamstow, E17. The phone had a short lead, but you could use it in every room. Gen got the biggest room by virtue of having to share it with a drum kit. Al's room was little bigger than a cupboard, and the small, single bed occupied just about every inch of the floor space. The bathroom wasn't large enough to house a proper bath, and so we installed a split-level, half-length tub that could only be sat in. Gen, the band's contortionist, could bend himself double in the deep end, making it look as though his feet were growing from his shoulders, and frankly, I think he was lucky he didn't drown in a ludicrous and embarrassing accident.

That winter was a particularly cold one and, of course, no central heating. I'd found a job half a mile from where I was born, building petrol-driven compressors. Working there meant I had to leave earlier than the other two, so it was my job to break the ice in the toilet. Although, thankfully, this was one water receptacle I didn't have to reach into afterwards.

We worked hard at getting gigs with little success, as with no local following, no promoter would take us. The gigs we did get were often pay-to-play—i.e. we paid something like £50 for "hire of the sound system" already installed. This was usually returnable if you brought in, say, fifty people—a figure way beyond us. Also, it's fair to say that we were terrible.

Al and Gen were both very competent, but my songwriting and singing were way off the mark. The music had no real direction. It was a mix of ideas and influences with no common theme or spirit, apart from one of desperation. Still, as ever, I kept writing and recording ideas into a Portastudio in my room, with the sound of Gen and Al's TV viewing next door coming clearly through the thin wall.

In search of a musical direction, we lured another ex-classmate to stay in our hideous abode and play keyboards with us; Al had come out of the closet and into a friend's house in Walthamstow. In the space of a couple of months, it had become clear that his addition to the band wasn't working, usually at the point when I began screaming. It wasn't that old corker "musical differences" but a clash of personalities: my brutal, bullying efficiency against his relaxed, lackadaisical aimlessness.

On the day he was late for the pick-up for a gig, we became a three piece again.

Among the friends we'd made in East London, we found another keyboard player, but after a couple of rehearsals in a warehouse in Wapping, he, too, created more excitement with the idea of him leaving than staying. This was the time of The Jesus and Mary Chain, R.E.M., The Smiths, and the birth of indie as we now think of it, of modern guitar rock.

Of course! We needed another guitarist!

The Irish Side

Soon after Gen and I gladly fled Walthamstow for Willesden, crossing the vast cultural divide between east and north-west London (our downstairs neighbour asked us on the way out, "What you wanna live on the Irish side for?" Her attitude pretty much answering her own question), we placed an ad in *Melody Maker* for a guitarist under the age of twenty-five. Although a fleeting mention of ability and possibly musical compatibility had been listed, a twenty-six-year-old would definitely have been ruled out.

We received two replies and confirmed two auditions. The first respondent was an overweight guy of Cypriot descent and didn't seem all that interested, which was fine by us. The second was a guy of Maltese descent—maybe Mediterraneans only read *Melody Maker* in those days. At the audition, the sound was as bad as it usually was in the dingy rehearsal room, where the mics always smelled of puke, so we couldn't hear a thing Jerry played. No matter, we needed a guitarist, and following in our tradition of useless auditions, he was in. As the months went by, he gradually revealed he'd lied to us about virtually everything asked in the advert, and to this day, I'm still confused as to exactly how old he is.

More rehearsals led to driving through the clashes of striking print workers and police in Wapping to gigs in Kentish Town, where the legendary Jon "Fat" Beast—a man largely (ho-ho) responsible for London's music scene in the late '80s— would put anyone onstage for twenty minutes and, uniquely, wouldn't ask for money in advance. He claims he still has old videos of us "wearing flares way before they were fashionable again," but as sartorially dubious as we often were, this is one claim I refute. Musically, things weren't as grim now either. I'd written a couple of songs that would appear on later Jesus Jones albums, and I had a growing interest in hip-hop and sampling.

I'd been a skateboarder at the end of the '70s and started again when we were living in Walthamstow. Skating was very underground then, and a good mix of cultures and classes. At Harrow, Chingford, or Meanwhile skateparks, often ghetto blasters would provide a soundtrack, helping me discover the Beastie Boys and Age of Chance around 1986.

I'd first heard about acid house from another skater in '88. That period was also probably the last time the British music press displayed any empathy with the spirit of rock 'n' roll, and via that, I discovered the likes of Sonic Youth, Big Black, and Public Enemy, as well as more eclectic sounds such as Les Mystere des Voix Bulgares. Musically, it was a diverse, creative, and exciting time—a time that encouraged experimenting.

It was also the age of Stock, Aitken, and Waterman's factory-line hit making, so it was by no means a simple, golden era, but enough originality was about to inspire me as I kept writing in my bedroom, aided now by the drum machine Jerry had borrowed from a friend, who later formed Renegade Soundwave.

Pandora's Digital Box

In May 1988, I saw an advert in *Loot* for a sampler for sale for £80. It turned out to be a glorified echo pedal with just two seconds maximum sampling time and no way of saving the input, but it was a revelation to me. I stayed awake until six in the morning, triggering parts of my record collection via the drum machine, just as I'd heard on all those hip-hop and house records. It felt like Christmas does to a five-year-old. It was a passport to another world of music, and I didn't hesitate for a moment to enter it.

For the next few months, I experimented with it, using the tape-speed control on the Portastudio to extend the sampling time of my box of joy, twisting the technology to try to get it to do the things I wanted. For a couple of years, I'd been an avid taper of radio stations, and any time I collected something good—a sound or a beat—I'd put the sampler to work on it.

An extra thrill existed to making music like this. It was still a new hybrid. Age of Chance had really jumped the gun and pretty much pioneered the new territory. I'd heard "There is No Love Between Us Anymore" by Pop Will Eat Itself on the radio, and they clearly had the right idea, but the press still had them stalled, temporarily, in the "grebo" dead-end category. The Shamen, on the other hand, I'd seen live a few times and felt they had got it all right—all the sounds of the new technology and, unlike Age of Chance, the tunes to match.

I had a good idea why they sounded so good live (which I later learned was totally incorrect) and changed our live setup accordingly. A form of sequencing so primitive that even London Underground engineers would have sneered now replaced Gen's bass drum. That gave us the ability to set up in ten minutes with a studio-perfect bass-drum sound, which, in a form of music led by that instrument—a concept most inhouse engineers couldn't understand at the time—was very important.

Comfortable

Although I was loving writing music more than ever, I was doing less and less about taking it anywhere. The stress of constantly making a nuisance of myself to get gigs the press never reviewed nor record companies saw—and sometimes didn't even have audiences—had worn me down. Plus, the rest of my life was good. I was getting good money at my job, and I was skating in most of my free time. I'd met Iain in a pub, recognised him as a skater by his Vision Street Wear shoes, and we'd started visiting skate parks around the country together. At this point, with our future keyboard player around, socially at least, Jesus Jones was born.

Gen saved us. He took on the manager role, targeting managers of bands we liked or who were successful at a lower level—and therefore people we thought we'd stand a chance with—and badgering them to take us on. He became in charge of getting us gigs too.

Jerry, meanwhile, had a friend who owned a time-share apartment in Spain and suggested we go there for a cheap holiday. He, Gen, and I would lie on the beach or get drunk in restaurants or watch Jerry's futile efforts with women and discuss what was happening, or what wasn't, with the band. Given that Gen and I would drag Jerry's unwilling, hungover form to the beach most days, where he'd lie face down in the sand, vomiting his breakfast of canned peaches, it's hard to credit his claim that Jerry and not me had invented the name *Jesus Jones*. However, we chose that name as part of our plan to totally overhaul the band and give it what I'm sure, subconsciously at least, was one last try.

It was also the time when I told them that if they gave me complete control, I knew how to make the best recording we could of some of the new songs. But which songs? Jerry insisted we include a song we had developed during the last six months: "Info Freako." I was totally against it. Gen must have swung it, because when we returned, we set about making this last stab recording with "Info Freako" as the first song.

Three months later, Gen took a half-finished version of the demo from my room. The first I knew about it was when I got a phone call from one Andy Ross, introducing himself as one of the two partners in Dave Balfe Management. He wanted to know if I knew they were also a record company—Food. And would I come in and meet them?

In December, we signed the deal: one single, with an option on another and an album. A few days later, we played a gig in Covent Garden to six Swedish au pairs, all of whom were friends of a woman I would marry eight months later. The gossip within the music industry travelled quickly—possibly 50/50 regarding the band and the au pairs—and the next gig we played, in January 1989, had a queue all the way around the block.

A month later, Food Records released "Info Freako," in its demo form, as the first Jesus Jones single, played on prime-time national radio and hotly tipped in the music press. It had been six-and-a-half years since I'd left school to become a rock star.

2.

"How does it feel to be one of the beautiful people?"

We'd put ourselves in the path of the tornado, and when it hit, it sucked us up, high above the ground. Since we proceeded to demolish large sections of America, I'll stick with that metaphor of cyclonic destruction. In retrospect, our ascent was rapid, but in the eye of the storm, it seemed very different. The more success we had, the more of it we envisioned, and we envisioned it happening a damn sight faster too. After years of effort, we wanted it all in a few months—we wanted fame like Russian miners had wanted a salary and felt just as justified in our demands.

Within weeks of signing the deal, we sold out gigs we could've busked outside a short while earlier. Our first reviews in the press appeared, and bigger and bigger articles and the strange thrill of photo shoots followed, which quickly became the usual tedium of photo shoots. In one such session, I learnt (but often later forgot) to never act the fool when the camera was around, since one brief moment of gurning—performed to ease the boredom when I thought we were between frames—became a postcard, which then appeared at every meet-the-fans moment everywhere around the world for the next six years. People even brought sketches of that damn card for me to sign.

Although I believed fervently in the music we were playing, I couldn't shake the feeling this whirlwind was just a huge confidence trick by Food and us, and that at any moment, the scenery would be dismantled, and a voice would say, "Alright lads, you've had your fun. Off you go." Unsurprisingly perhaps, I've never felt that much in common with Charles Aznavour, but he really hit the mark when he said, "Success is the result of a collective hallucination stimulated by the artist." That feeling increased rather than diminished with time and greater success.

Our sense of unreality was heightened when we had to leave our jobs to do our first tours, supporting two bands we greatly admired: first The Shamen and then The Wonder Stuff. We toured on our own with two itineraries: the gigs in the evening, the skateparks in the day.

Food released a trio of Jesus Jones singles, all of which, with unerring accuracy, just missed the Top 40—this was in an age when indie bands would be front-page music-press news if they peaked at #35 for a week. This frustrated me hugely. How dare people not buy our records?

Food released our first album, *Liquidizer*, a year after their first contract had been proffered, and it did respectably, entering the Top 40 but many places lower than I felt it belonged. I was maniacal enough to believe that success was our due, that the progress we'd had with tours, press, and records was inevitable, and the fact we hadn't had more success by this point was an irritation.

By the end of 1989, we had a manager, I had a publishing deal, Gen had a huge file of press clippings in his diary—some of which were very complimentary, we could get on the guest list of any gig in town, we'd supported our peers on tour, and people recognised me when I went out. Embarrassing as it is to admit, this was a dream come true.

I was becoming famous!

"It's a long way to the top if you wanna rock 'n' roll"

If I was at home, I was writing. Even during the recording of *Liquidizer*, I was writing before I went into the studio every day, mostly because Food were releasing songs as fast as I could write and record them—a notion exists that a band's second album is the "difficult" one. Although, within the industry, that has stretched to the "difficult third" and often fourth. With this work schedule, I feel we had a difficult first album too.

As Food was releasing the first album, I was writing the songs for the second, some of which were recorded at the start of 1990 just before we toured again; first in Romania—one month after the revolution, when the country was still volatile enough for us to require a massive military escort for our last gig—and then in a ludicrously mismatched tour with The Cramps as they played to their strictly partisan fans all over Europe. In southern France and Spain, we felt as though we were on holiday, and the audiences were open-minded and receptive. In the north, the crowds were openly hostile, jeering, spitting, and throwing cans and bottles. In Italy, they threw lira coins, which was far more effective than trying to spend that feeble denomination.

Every night we knew what was coming, but we stuck it out with the certainty that once we got home, the songs we'd recorded and cut for our second album, *Doubt*, would be hits. And they were.

Our winning streak started in April 1990, and during the next three years, we'd tally six Top-40 hits and two Top-10 albums, one of which entered at #1. Most of Europe ignored us by and large, but we had hits in Switzerland, Japan, South Africa, New Zealand, Canada, and, rumour has it, Poland.

Most importantly, *Doubt* became a huge hit in the US—a million-unit selling album—and that brought real fame.

By now it was impossible to travel, shop, or go out without being embarrassed by the attention I'd receive. Sometimes gangs of schoolkids yelled at me, sometimes Japanese tourists burst into tears because of my presence, and most embarrassing of all, sometimes groups of builders sang my songs at me. I should inform the world that the famous are not, in fact, deaf and blind. Although the many people who pointed and talked loudly about me clearly assumed so. If you've ever wondered what it's like to be an animal in a zoo, I can tell you—even if my knowledge is limited through never having flung my own dung at spectators or copulated openly in public.

My phone number was still listed, and I started receiving nuisance calls. Women sent me their underwear in the post. I was constantly doing interviews and photo sessions, and my presence in the media was such that one thoughtless, throwaway, derogatory remark about a popular boy band of the time resulted in many months of hate mail, including death threats from an eight-year-old in the Seychelles.

I didn't get a bodyguard.

"You guys rock!"

Fame was different in America, partly because of our greater success there and partly because, in my experience, the American attitude towards fame is different from the rest of the world's. It's more admired, certainly more respected than in the UK or Australia where it is the eighth deadly sin—as soul troubling as lust. The downside to this is that the cause of the fame is largely irrelevant. Where else in the world could a serial killer have a fan club?

So, while we would do in-store signings with large queues around the block, the queuers would often arrive at our table and, with a disinterested glance, mutely proffer a torn till receipt from McDonalds for all five of us to sign—a situation where being "Gen" rather than "Jerry de Borg" was a great advantage. On its own, this was still a great improvement from building petrol-driven compressors for a living, but in conjunction with the meet-and-greets after every gig—the America-only convention of having the town's music industry come and be introduced to you after the show, thrusting a promo copy of the single at you and saying things like, "You're Brian, aren't you? I love that song of yours. What's it called?"— bits of my soul were being chipped away. Other members of the band were enviably pragmatic in dealing with this: take coke and enjoy talking shit all night.

One particular lowlight for me was exiting the tour bus in San Francisco, after a few hours of terrible sleep following a gig in Los Angeles, to have a staggering drunk confront me with a camera pointing at me and shouting, "Hey! Asshole! Lemme take your picture." He summed it up for me. *I hate you but wait 'til my friends see I met a famous guy!*

Despite the occasional query as to which one of us was Jesus, this really was the dream come to life. The truth is that, overall, being a famous rock star was just as glamorous as I'd hoped and contained absolutely everything it should have. By which I mean:

Sex ...

From almost the first tour, it became apparent that if you wanted it, sex was easily available. I was married, and I didn't want it, but that didn't stop it coming at me. We'd be backstage in Texas and the security guard would say, "This chick outside says she's here to blow the band. Do I let her in?" Our soundman would meet us at soundcheck and say, "Two girls outside bet me ten dollars they'd 'do that singer tonight'." Five dollars each? What an insult!

In America, Japan, and Australia, women would literally throw themselves at us, and they wouldn't always be thrown back. At instore signings, girls would lift their shirts and say, "Sign these. And do you guys wanna come to a party afterwards?" Jerry, ever the artist, developed a signature technique for these occasions, the *O* in his surname neatly encircling a nipple.

Then a woman in a micro dress strode up to me as I lounged on a dressing room sofa and demanded I sign her breast. Two minutes later, she returned to command me to sign her upper thigh, placing a leg on the sofa arm and hiking up her dress to reveal she'd traded her underwear for a backstage pass. In another two minutes, she returned, swung her backside to me, bent double, and insisted I perform one more unsteady squiggle, all of which did us no end of good with the radio station manager sitting next to me.

When the band didn't accept the offers, the crew swept up, and at least one instance occurred of such depravity it made me wonder about these women—people who would subject themselves to such humiliation and initiate acts seemingly not of enjoyment but of desperation. Great acrobatics though.

...and Drugs

From the first tour, it became apparent that if you wanted them, they were easily available. This isn't really saying much, since drugs have been a cornerstone of youth culture for as long as youth culture has existed, just in case no-one has noticed. And who knows, maybe slightly before too. But the influence of acid house made drug taking far more acceptable to much more of the population, unless a historical precedent exists for half a million Britons on E every weekend that I'm unaware of.

No shadowy evil figure hovered in our background, waiting to pervert our innocence. Instead, just the same sort of people—friends of friends—who'd always dealt to the casual users in the band hung around. Only, we had more friends around the world now. Instances of free drugs for all were few, if memorable. Although being offered cocaine at $4 a gram in Brazil almost qualifies.

I was still endorsing and enforcing the "only play straight" rule from years prior, which seems draconian but made a lot of sense for us—playing music driven by the mathematically precise rhythms of sequencers meant that any deviation in timing was glaringly obvious, and instead of imbuing us with the spirit of jazz, it made us sound like an orchestra jumping from a train. Maybe I just don't dig jazz, man.

Our exuberance on stage frequently got the better of us, and the truth is that we were never the slickest band anyhow, hence no drink or drugs onstage. You'd be fit enough to play properly, or you were out, a ruling that had me ridiculed in the press as "The Cliff Richard of indie" (it was the "indie" part that I bridled at)—a prejudice reinforced by my not endorsing drugs in print, unlike many contemporaries of ours, some of whom developed a reputation that dwarfed their music. Again, a fear of being hidden in the masses made me kick out at the rigid conformity of repeating tales of narcotic abandon, toeing the sub-textual line that insisted drug taking equalled creativity—a notion the press wholly endorsed until some poor sod OD'd.

Out of the eye of the press, having slightly better access to narcotics than most of the population, the band sampled the entire gamut of street drugs. Some just experimented with, others used more regularly, but none of us became drug users to the point where it infringed on the band or our social lives. The inevitable, occasional bad experiences transpired, but if ever a drug existed that could have tripped us up, it was alcohol.

As a contemporary of ours put it at the time, we were just doing the things that most people our age were doing.

... & Rock 'N' Roll

The best bit! We played music we believed in, music that moved us emotionally and physically, and we enjoyed the full rock 'n' roll experience—tiny club gigs full of raw energy and noise, blood-covered strings in London and Osaka, guitars rusting from sweat in over-full and inhumanely humid shows in Sydney, New Orleans, and Valencia, frustration and trashed equipment in Minneapolis, winning over the crowd at festivals in Finland and Denmark, being the unexpected revelation at the bottom of the bill in Rio de Janeiro and Amsterdam, selling out 10,000 seaters in the US, playing on while the audience leapt up and down with such force the stage crew had to hold down the PA while the floor collapsed, amps and samplers blowing up, stage invasions, dying onstage in Germany, fans knocking the mike into my face and chipping my teeth as they climbed onstage, my left leg shaking uncontrollably as we played to 72,000 people at Wembley Stadium—rediscovering stage fright, hearing an audience drown out the band with their singing, and us carrying on however we could while seeing a sea of clapping hands and smiling faces in front of us on nearly every continent on the planet and controlling that with a gesture or a word.

There would be times I'd stand back and watch Alan, ever the image of a rock god, his head swinging madly over his bass as though it would fly off at any moment; Jerry, eyes closed, head back and legs apart, a gold Gibson Les Paul in his hands, sweat pouring down his shirtless figure, a girl in the crowd clutching his leg and staring at him, mouth open; Iain, transformed from the urbane and charming into an eruption of violence and lunacy, trashing his keyboard with such aggression that people frequently insisted, wrongly, that he could only be miming. And then, occasionally, I'd look at Gen behind the drum kit and he'd catch my eye. Sometimes it was simultaneous, other times not, but we'd be thinking, "We did it! After all this time, we're living the dream, here on this huge rock-n-roll stage in front of this huge rock-n-roll audience."

We lived the dream. By 1993 and our third album, we woke up.

3.

Be Careful What You Dream, It May Come True

Perverse was our third album and a title I'd probably been looking for most of my life as a musician. Written at the end of 1991 and early 1992, it was a good opportunity to try and distance us further from the majority of rock bands with whom I felt little empathy. In fashion terms, the idea of mixing rock music with a still growing number of forms of dance music was over—meaning '60's retro rock bands no longer took their record company's advice on who should remix them—but in its absence was, to my mind, a vacuum—a non-era that offered a return to the past in one of two choices: grunge or Britpop. I was baffled that clearly exciting and inventive alternatives existed, sounds that invoked the spirit of classic rock 'n' roll, as typified by The Prodigy's first album in 1992.

I couldn't understand why the rock press, in what I still consider to be its nadir, was incessantly eulogising offensively plagiaristic bands, while many nights of the week I'd be in the centre of a riotous dance floor, hearing exhilarating sounds, the like of which I'd never heard before, sounds completely and deliberately ignored by the medium I'd always expected to keep me informed. The contrast between the preservers of the status quo and the adventurers made it an embarrassing time to be seen with a guitar in public.

The way I envisaged Jesus Jones riding the dividing line, still our *raison d'être*, was by attempting to make a modern rock album in the way I thought a bedroom techno musician would approach it. Subsequently, we wrote the album entirely on computer—instruments played in via keyboards, midi-guitars, or a midi-drum kit. The discs were then handed to our producer who manipulated it further, and I sang over the results. I even tried to find a way of producing the songs without any human singing at all; thankfully, laziness got the better of me, and I stood in the vocal booth mechanically unaided.

Perverse is a very dark-sounding album, but I think our finest hour—an opinion shared by many who know and like the band. Three things dictated the tone: a constant aural diet of minor-key techno, the rampaging doom of Sonic Youth, and tapes of traditional Lebanese songs—staggeringly powerful music but beautiful in the way that diamorphine is useful.

The second key ingredient was the depression I'd slumped into at the start of 1991—a state of mind it took me four years to get out of, a reaction to my fame. It's not hard to imagine always having people look at you and talk about you within plain view results in at least a trace of paranoia. More than this was that I was supposed to be enjoying myself, and I wasn't.

Fame was what I had wanted for most of my life, and now I had developed an allergy to it. Or, as I wrote on the album, *"The problem with success is you become what you detest."* Given that the cardinal social sin of people who have something enviable is to complain about it, I bottled it up and continued telling the world how great life was. (Students of psychiatry may wish to place a reference mark here *.)

A manifestation of my altered state of mind was that the rest of my life was chaotic and extreme. At one point in '92, I clubbed every night of the week, drank heavily, and was usually amongst the last to leave, all of which seemed entirely normal. Ironically, as my fame faded, I lived like the rock star of legend but doing less of what that is really about—creating music.

The pressures of being the self-appointed leader and spokesman—meaning I only had myself to blame—were also building up. Whereas, in 1989, I could write music all day long, in 1992, I spent half of every day doing interviews or providing quotes for music papers, magazines, and radio stations around the world. I didn't mind this—I still really enjoyed it—but learning Korean for "*Hello*" in front of a DAT recorder while a motorbike courier waited outside didn't help me link a verse to a chorus. And, of course, all that didn't leave long before the clubs opened.

Delegating promotion to other members of the band—those prepared to do it—almost worked, but once I'd established myself as the accepted spokesman, people came to expect, and occasionally demanded, to hear me.

Most crucially, signs of our waning popularity weighed on my mind. A few gigs we expected to sell out that didn't alongside the standard-issue massacring in the press gave me a feeling that somehow the atmosphere had changed. The belief that the fame we had received was inevitable became replaced with constant doubts about my abilities and worth.

Me: "Let's not take things for granted. We shouldn't expect everything to go our way this time."

Record Company Guy: "No, sure. Our conservative estimate for this album is three- to- four-million sales."

Soon after the release of *Perverse*, it became apparent the album wouldn't have the same success as *Doubt*. Our UK tour pretty much held its own, but our success now seemed like thin ice in late spring. As speed skaters, that wasn't good. The US was much the same. Although, in the further flung parts of the tour, we suffered some low attendances. The morale on tour seemed okay at the time but having heard from fans who had attended those shows, it appeared we weren't the live band we had been anymore.

We had made an album that defied the fashion of the time, and now fashion stared us down. Creatively, I felt I had little option, but it was a disastrous career move to attempt the unusual in a time of rigid conservatism. U2 had attempted the same move around the same time with *Achtung Baby* and even then, many years and many albums into a far more successful career than ours, they staggered a little before they recovered some time later. With just one fair-sized success, we had greasy hands on the slippery ladder to success, and what's more, some bastard was pouring boiling oil on us.

Nowhere was this more obvious than in America, where even the word *techno* had people rolling their eyes, wailing, gnashing their teeth, speaking in tongues, and writing derogatory articles with the word "disco" featured in them. If Sonic Youth were to be believed and 1991 really was "the year punk rock broke," expecting the next musical revolution to be accepted just two years later was more than optimistic.

"Yes, but," you may ask, "was the album any good?"

Well, once you've shown me the empirical device for measuring that, I'll tell you.

All in all, my life, career, and marriage were all breaking down.

> "Again, again, again, again, again, again, again, again. Why don't we do it, why don't we do it again?"
> Status Quo

Here's a good ruse, one to remind the wearying reader that life in a rock band is, after all, easy and glamorous: persuading promotions staff from other EMI branches to invite you to their countries for "work" (i.e. talking about yourself in a five-star hotel with all expenses paid).

By the time we had finished touring for *Perverse*, it was autumn '93, and as a number of South American branches of EMI had happily accepted our suggestion—although not as gleefully as we packed our bags—I got the opportunity to visit Mexico City and Uruguay and return to Argentina and Brazil in their late spring. Our part of the deal was to do interviews, some hasty photo shoots (the best kind), and occasionally the odd mime on TV. And I mean *odd*, too. I've seen and appeared on kid's TV shows around the world, but the strangest are in South America, where the band often must share stage space with cast members who are frequently in some sort of costume. Of course, the band are never told this in advance, which leads to tense moments. I shall never forget being filmed in a studio in the outskirts of Rio de Janeiro and turning around at the end of the song to see Jerry wrestling with a midget in a crocodile suit. This had not been what I envisaged as a nine-year-old.

Returning home with a significantly less suntan than the rest of the band, I started writing the fourth album. It's also significant that I remember the birth of my daughter interrupting my clubbing rather than my writing, and it pains me to say that. Writing wasn't getting any easier, and subconsciously, I know now I was avoiding it. I was proud of what I had written so far for the next album, although it had to be wrenched out, and for the first time in years, I didn't have a definite direction. Rock music was still creatively unambitious, and dance music had paused briefly before the respite with drum 'n' bass.

After a year of painstaking creation, I presented twelve songs to the record company and management in a meeting at Food's office in Camden. It was there where I first received that well-worn music industry line, "This is fine, but where are the singles?" That meant writing more songs, about sixteen I reckoned.

Leaving the meeting by way of lighter conversation, my manager said, "Apparently, the most stressful times in life are moving home, getting divorced, and going on holiday."

I pondered that, having just moved out from my wife and daughter that morning and was about to go to my new home to pack for a Japanese tour the next day ... and with another album to write. The only worse time in my life was returning from that tour.

Six months later, Food okayed my sixteen new songs. We tried a demo recording with two producers, Iain Richardson and Nick Coler, which, with much impatient pushing from me, they cleared us to start recording the pick of the twenty-eight songs amassed.

It was summer 1995 and things were looking up. The studio sessions were fun and easy—five days a week, eight to ten hours a day—and I had started a new relationship, and not only could I read of a new club opening and not inexplicably find myself at the bar hours later, but I was getting properly fit, riding to and from the studio in preparation for a long mountain bike trip.

The "B" Word

I'd cycled around London in the band's heyday because it was the perfect way of getting everywhere on time whilst avoiding the tube-bound, singing builders' embarrassment. I'd also become neurotic with the idea that being fit would help my singing and prevent me from losing my voice at gigs, like those well-known fitness fanatics: Janis Joplin, Billie Holiday, Jim Morrison, Kurt Cobain, Iggy Pop, and Robert Plant. Had I known about warming up before a gig, I'd be a fat slob with a beautiful voice today.

However, I got more and more into mountain biking, going abroad on several biking holidays, and at the start of '95, I had booked a trip that involved cycling from Lhasa in Tibet to Nepal's capitol, Kathmandu, by way of the base camp at the north face of Everest. It seemed to me that I couldn't get further away from endlessly writing music and compulsive clubbing than shivering in a tent at 18,000 feet in the Himalaya. The trip's other purpose as a celebration of finishing the album became less and less likely as the recording stretched on.

Completing the recording after four months—twice as long as *Perverse*—Food had to persuade me that mixing the entire album in the few days before I left was not conducive to good results, as if several twenty-four-hour sessions in a row might not work out!

Tibet was perfect. I got saddle sores, sunburn, fatigue, dysentery, "mild" altitude sickness, and worst of all, grew a beard. Well, a sort-of beard. Once again, I spent twenty-four hours a day with a small group of people, none of whom killed me or each other, even after a month. Although it came close on a couple of occasions. I rode a sixteen-mile dirt-road climb, starting at 12,000 feet and ending at 15,000—one of the many long roads over high-altitude desert passes, sometimes to 18,000 feet above sea level. But there was always the descent afterwards.

We visited the Dalai Lama's palace—the Potala—but the current tenants weren't keen on having anything more than photos of him present, this being "The autonomous region of Tibet, People's Republic of China." The Chinese government was not big on irony. I got to stand at the foot of Everest, my head exploding with the pain of far-too-little oxygen, looking 10,000 feet up that wall of black rock and ice, and knowing my ambitions (thank God!) lie elsewhere. At base camp, the South Korean team had lost two men to the mountain and the Spanish team before them three more.

We spent a day dropping from the Tibetan plateau at 18,000 feet (I clocked the second fastest speed at 45mph), across the landslides, and over the narrow, gorge-side road to the Nepalese valleys where, at 2,000 feet with all that unaccustomed oxygen, I felt like the Superman of the knobbly tyred world. The only resurgence of anxiety I felt was when one of our party attempted to play a tape of R.E.M. and The Pixies in the Chinese van we sometimes travelled in. I felt happier on my getaway hearing the driver's tape of Szechwan folk songs, even if they did sound like a tone-deaf village idiot accompanying himself with a rubber band on a stick.

Two weeks after I returned home, the album was mixed. Then rejected. Food didn't think the production was "right." After the sense of crushing disappointment, my main feeling was relief at Food's insistence that I didn't need to write any more songs. Even if we had to re-record—including home demos, this would be the third time for me—at least those days of staring out the window and agonising over filling the blank verses with words I'd hate the next day were over.

The start of 1996 marked the third anniversary of the release of *Perverse*—our last album. I stopped worrying about the gap. There didn't seem any point now. What really mattered was just to get the bloody thing done, to have friends and family ask, "So, what are you up to now?" without flinching at the reply.

A suggestion came for a trial recording with EMI UK's then-managing director. The fact the suggestion came from EMI UK's then-managing director didn't necessarily rule it out, so we tried it. It didn't work. We searched for another producer, and I met one our manager suggested. We gave him a tape, and after a month of unreturned phone calls, we took that as a *no*. Food and EMI's suggestions amounted to a very small list, and after a few practicalities were discussed, like "No, we haven't got £2,000,000," the list couldn't have gotten any smaller.

What I'd like to describe again as perversity but in this case is stupidity, meant that we'd never used the same producer twice, even in the case of Martyn Phillips, who had produced the single that had been #1 on all but one of USA's four major charts in 1991, "Right Here, Right Now." When his name made a triumphal return in our minds, the self-recriminating slapping of foreheads was thunderous. Even better, he was prepared to do it, after he'd finished his current project ... in June!

from Tokyo to Bwcfa

It was well beyond time to be a real band again. We rehearsed, briefed our agent, and went on a small, unannounced tour of England, with a quick flirtation with Wales. Preparation time was short, the gigs were small, morale was pretty low, and too much expectation surrounded these tiny gigs from us and from the fans who'd waited years to see us in grander surroundings. I think we were pretty scrappy. We'd made a point of having a road manager, but we did not employ any other crew at all, so we had to lift all our own gear before and after gigs.

Our previous tour, eighteen months before, had ended with a support slot, two nights running at a sold-out Tokyo Budokan. It was a game attempt to try and rediscover the fire from our early shows, but it didn't really work, and the joy of playing live again soon gave way to the defeat of sitting in traffic jams on English motorways.

In the studio, the tour had at least given us a sense of purpose, and playing songs for the album live had enabled us to hear the songs in a new light, something we needed by now. My aim had been to record the band live in the studio—a totally different approach from our other albums—but Martyn's decision was to go for a 50/50 mix of live performance bolted on to electronica, our cyborg approach once more. Choosing him as producer, in my mind, meant allowing him to follow his vision.

I didn't regret the decision, as the sessions proved very different from the previous recording a year before and turned out very well. However, it was painstaking work; Martyn's perfectionism was beyond that of anyone I'd worked with before, including myself.

*

Exit Bond Man

By September, we'd done little in the way of finished songs, getting three quarters of the
way through a track and then moving on to another, returning to do a little more in a week or so before moving on again. We entered a different time zone wherein it was possible to end a day's work with not much more than different bass and snare drum sounds.

Alan had moved to his wife's home town of Chicago and had to fly over whenever we needed him to play bass, although we were organised enough to ensure his regular, daily commute wasn't a trans-Atlantic one. In the meantime, he led a life separate to the band and was in pursuit of the astonishing transformation from the Wild Man of Rock into the Mild Man of DIY. Reassuringly, Jerry would still receive the occasional, semi-coherent and rambling phone call at 5:30 a.m. on a Chicago morning.

Iain and Jerry would visit the studio often, usually just to see how things were progressing and sometimes for a performance. By eight at night, the lure of the pub, or simply the boredom of observing multiple knob twiddling, drew them from the building. I was present all day, every day, to make decisions on any changes and sometimes to sing or play guitar.

Gen seemed to feel the time drag more than anyone else. He'd been trying for a couple of years to be more involved in the band and the album, but there just didn't seem to be the right channel for that extra energy. Unless anyone else in the band could write a potential single in its entirety, they had just about nothing to do before the studio sessions started and not that much afterwards. Instead, he'd directed his efforts elsewhere, playing with a couple of other bands, even touring America with one. He became increasingly distant, rarely giving opinions on the recordings and only then under pressure. Both bands he played with needed a full-time drummer, and Gen, probably the most proficient player in the band, was well worth enticing. No-one was surprised when he told us he wanted to leave. He'd had the signpost up for long enough.

Although I knew what was coming and was aware of the enormity of losing seventeen years of struggle and success together, I didn't feel able to stop it. So much of my life was consumed with finishing the album. So much of my concentration focussed on making it as good as it could be, not cutting any of the corners that would be unforgivable after all the time between releases. I wasn't constantly in the middle of vocal or guitar takes or manning the mixing console from sunrise to sunset, but after three difficult years, the recording had become an obsession that dominated my mind.

All the drum parts were done, and Gen no longer needed to be in the studio, but the album was still less than half done and was at the point where I had to present Food with a tape of what we'd done so far to get their approval to continue; if they didn't like it, we'd be where we were two years previously. It was a crisis point twice over, and I couldn't cope with both dilemmas.

I knew Gen leaving was a huge blow and that it would hit me later, but meanwhile, the grindstone remained spinning. What *did* surprise me was Gen had been the first to leave. I'd felt that fuses would be smouldering ever since Food's rejection of the first recordings. The pressure of hanging around, waiting to see if we still had a career or not, was as bad for the rest of the band as it was for me, only they didn't have the same power to affect that as I did or the distraction of being deeply involved with the album every day. Whilst I wrote and oversaw the recordings, they had to kill time their own way, and with my memories of the dole, I can say that after the first month that isn't the fun that it might sound.

Gen wasn't the only one who had other opportunities. Alan got regular gigs in Chicago with his other band, The Waco Brothers, and possibilities seemed to be there for the other two also. Gen just seemed to reach the end of the line first because his frustration could be soothed away instantaneously, willing arms ready and able to ease the transfer, no change in lifestyle to muddy the pool. I know, too, he wasn't convinced with what was coming from the studio. The potential for working on those same songs for the rest of our lives—or until the money ran out—hardly helped. And I have no doubt it was refreshing to be out of my shadow. Who could blame him? Not us.

We got the go-ahead from Food and The Album—now an epic requiring capitals—ground on relentlessly becoming an insatiable organism that needed most of my time and all my consciousness to feed it, like a berserk parking meter. I told people it was like the First World War; it'd all be finished by Christmas. That rebounded on me like it rebounded on the British Generals, only I didn't shoot Gen at dawn for desertion.

My daughter turned three, and I'd never released an album in her lifetime. She told her mum my job was working on computers, and when she was old enough to understand that I did something similar to the Spice Girls, she'd ask, "Is that you singing?" whenever I'd put on a record. I think my Prada skirt and high-heeled boots confused her, but then it's good to feel glamorous when doing the household chores.

When it became clear we had no chance of finishing the album by the end of 1996, I decided to take off a couple of weeks and see in the new year in New York.

4.

Back to the Beginning— January 1997

January, the month when the good intent of a boozy Christmas develops mechanical problems and is grounded, sitting on the runway, waiting for clearance from reality. I flew back from New York, feeling like Mussolini looking at a train timetable, and if I had an automobile analogy to complete the trio of transport images, I'd show me in the driving seat, careening into 1997, fiercely resolute and defiantly optimistic.

My girlfriend stayed home in New York. She'd come to the UK on a tourist visa, and after eighteen months, it got harder to convince immigration she still had sights to see. Plus, she'd had enough of the high misery quotient in British people (she lived with me through much of this album, who could blame her?), got disorientated by TV programmes running for more than three minutes without adverts, and simply wasn't used to such comparatively low levels of greenhouse gas emission from a nation. Our Dr. Pepper tasted inferior too; some things are worth taking a stand on. We didn't break up, we just kept American Airlines in profit for a few years, my girlfriend shouldering most of the jet lag.

I returned doing exactly what I had done before Christmas, like the rest of the non-turkey population. Not that returning to Martyn's in-house studio was a chore. In fact, I enjoyed the routine of cycling five days a week, swearing at incompetent motorists with righteous fury on the way, Martyn's girlfriend—Owzlem—feeding me exquisite food, writing emails incessantly, and every so often, being asked to comment on a mix.

All the recording was done, and the studio time was spent with Martyn employing his formidable arsenal of sound-manipulating computer equipment to create weird aural spectres around the performances the band had made months earlier. Recording at Martyn's house was never the archetypal studio session. Unlike the images of studios from music videos, the control room hogged most of the space, not the performance area. We had done all the singing or drumming or guitar playing individually in a single ten-foot-by-ten-foot room while Martyn sat behind the mixing desk in an area twice that size.

With the recording finished, Martyn stayed in the control room, and I spent most of the day at the kitchen table, only entering the studio to check how the weird sample of the backing vocals progressed or what Alan's chopped-up bass line now did for the song. The refinements to the songs became slighter and slighter, so we were obviously getting closer to the end. However, we definitely worked with the maxim that a work of art is never finished, merely abandoned, and so a momentous completion was never achieved, just deferred. For example, "The Next Big Thing"—the song that would be the first single from the album—while not needing any more recording work, had twenty-four mixes to choose from.

Say, "frozen cheese"

As January gained momentum, rolling into the new year, the machinery behind our re-launch started up. Artwork suggestions came in from the designers. I went to meetings at Food's office to see photographer's portfolios. And we met with Michelle, our stylist for *Perverse*. By the end of the month, we had planned the album's artwork photo sessions and our press photos.

The first session was a location shoot near St. Austell, Cornwall. I hired a car and picked up the rest of the band, noting that first Alan and then Iain had joined me in the freshly dyed blond look. We nodded our blond heads through the five-hour drive, listening to the Eels, Daft Punk, Blur, and bending the doors out of shape with drum 'n' bass.

We got to the hotel at about 1 a.m. The rooms had no heating, but the temperature was still a degree or two above freezing, so clearly only soft, dyed-blond jessies from up London way would need that sort of thing. No-one slept, and we had to relinquish the pretence of doing so at 6 a.m. anyway. Inevitably, we rushed through breakfast and getting made up so we could sit around doing nothing for a couple of hours—Bill Wyman's Law, as it is now known. At least the temperature had risen a couple of degrees with the daylight.

When we did finally leave the hotel, things got much worse. The location was a Cornish tin mine, high on a hill above the town with a clear view of the sea. The clear view meant nothing would stop the howling wind swooping from the English Channel and tearing up the hill, where it savaged the already feeble ambient temperature with a razor-edged wind chill. We were dressed in light summer suits: thin silk shirts with delicate, open jackets. Even above the noise of the gale, you could hear Jerry's teeth chattering. I couldn't move my face muscles properly, and my sleep-deprived panda eyes allied with my physiognomical rictus would have made Picasso scream in inspired horror. Animal nature came to the fore as we jostled aggressively to shelter behind each other, only to be ordered by the photographer to spread out again. The makeup woman worked her powders to the tin bottoms, trying to conceal teary eyes and running noses.

Looking like a collection of well-styled Quasimodos wasn't really the way we wanted to appear on our great comeback, so we moved location out of the wind a little, but we were still stupidly clad for a typical January. Our saviour was the early fading of light. By five o'clock, we drove home with the car heater on full until we reached the other side of Devon—a selection of eerily lit photos of us in *Dr. Who* scenery in the can.

The next day wasn't a lot better. Working with the same photographer, we met at EMI's Hammersmith office early in the morning. The idea for the shoot was a brilliant one. A van had been hired and decorated like a garish living room—purple walls and green floor. The van's rear door remained up, and the photographer was harnessed inside the van directly behind the driver. In this way, we'd drive around West London, sitting in our neon living room, with a variety of grey suburbs and busy roads as our ever-changing backdrop. It looked great, but it was still just as cold, and we had the same feeble clothes on. Also, we tried to lounge about, looking indifferent while the van swung around corners at 50mph with the back open. Several times we nearly became a three piece, and a solo career was nearly built on three mangled corpses strewn across the A40. If hypothermia didn't get us before the traffic did.

5.

FEBRUARY

After a weekend of being warm—unless you raced mountain bikes, as I did—we had another shoot with a different photographer. Ah, the warm luxury of a studio shoot! The same formula is used on all studio shoots. The photographer arranges the band—after they've hung around for a couple of hours, of course—and takes a Polaroid to check the lights, positions, etc. This shot is the cue for the release of hours of frustration at waiting, and a riot of puerile gurning ensues.

Iain, in particular, could muster a face-busting gargoyle impression that would have been a far more daunting defence on a mediaeval castle than mere burning oil. Jerry collected as many of these Polaroids as he could and now has a collection that can curdle milk while it's still in the cow.

The next and final day of press and album shots were done in the cold again, shooting inside the disused town hall in Bethnal Green. The heating did work, but the owner wouldn't let us use it. Perhaps he was from Cornish hotelier stock. It was colder inside the building than out.

By now you should have the impression we were entirely used to this sort of irony on photo shoots.

The End! (nearly)

As I got numb for the camera, Martyn had continued working. He would probably still be working on our album if we hadn't pointed out we'd soon have the artwork, press shots, and release date done without actually having the music.

On February 7, 1997, we celebrated the album's completion in a Soho bar. A few days later we did actually finish.

There it was, over three years of my span on Earth preserved on two-inch tape and an Apple Macintosh hard drive. The bane of my existence but the reason for getting up every day, sometimes a testament to the joy of creating music and sometimes a diary of some of the worst times in my life, captured on such flimsy media and later available for £14 or even less in a sale. What a bargain.

For over a year, I'd been communicating with Jesus Jones fans via an internet site in Australia. Periods of inactivity from the band left little for the chat group to discuss, and so a regular contest of "What should the album be called?" had arisen. *Strawberry* and *Aluminium* were a couple of suggestions, but when, at the close of one such bulletin-board discussion, "Here's the damn album already!" cropped up, that was the title for me. (Thanks, Darren.)

I liked it because it wasn't the archetypal, one-word, meaningful title we'd had before. I liked the irreverence too. For about three days, it was the official title of the album, until caution and the awareness it wouldn't be that amusing to the world at large caused furrowed brows at the offices of Food and EMI. I returned to an archetypal, one-word meaningful title: *Already.*

On Valentine's Day, I attempted to rekindle my long-lost romance with the press. Jerry and I met a journalist Food had hired to interview us and would submit a press release from the resulting transcription. I'd always enjoyed interviews, apart from American Top 40 radio stations, where being asked how we got the name (126 times on one six-week tour) sedated me instantly. I was not from the "the music does the talking, man" school since I discovered its language didn't always translate accurately and its quotes made for short articles. Given a decent cup of coffee or a little provocation—anything with a question mark—I could rattle off for hours. My only problem was remembering anecdotes in front of a tape recorder, in the same way that entering a supermarket immediately clears your mind of the most important item on your shopping list. So, I babbled, Jerry supported, EMI paid the cafe bill, and soon afterwards, an insider prepared a document to re-introduce us to the press, written in their own style. In retrospect, I think the money would have been better spent on letter bombs.

Already was cut—transformed from a recording to a master copy. Cutting engineers are the ultimate hi-fi snobs of the world. They can tell you what green sounds like. They can hear what make of tape you used to record. They name their kids after brands of amplifiers (probably). I think it's either a huge con trick by a self-protecting industry or evidence of an unusual branch of human evolution.

My approach in the cutting room was mainly to wait until the levels moved into the red and then say I liked it. Martyn was in his element with the engineer, and while they discussed levels of kilohertz, I looked out the second-floor cutting room's floor-to-ceiling window at the trees and the clouds and the traffic of West London, and I listened to those songs once again.

Sometimes I'd get a little fizz of excitement, a distant relative of the feeling I'd had writing the song, thinking, *Yes! It still moves me, even now!* Some songs would make me feel like our future was golden and guaranteed. How could anyone with a beating heart deny this? A key change, a piece of singing, a bass line could leap out and let me know it had all been worthwhile. Occasionally, I'd hear a song and find it hard to believe I'd written it, when it flowed with such accomplishment and unfamiliar movement that its strangeness refuted any knowledge of me. Sometimes I couldn't wait for a song to finish—moments of acute discomfort at a phrasing or a verse, hoping no-one was really paying attention. What was I thinking with a cheesy guitar line like that? Sometimes I'd wish I'd done more or less or shut up or insisted or compromised or experimented or just scrapped it and started all over again.

It's always that way at the cut.

6.

MARCH

Still the album wouldn't lie down. Martyn, possibly distracted by talk of a particularly interesting frequency with the engineer, decided it wasn't quite right. The transfer from his computer to the studio's had involved a sixteen-bit process instead of a twenty-bit process and, sonically, this just would not do. I didn't stay to examine the four-bit difference.

I went to work on what would become the best promotion the album got—the Jesus Jones website. A friend and I had created a site to rival a couple of existing ones a year or so before, the division of labour split with me doing most of the design and him doing the technical stuff. The site was overdue for an overhaul as the talk of the forthcoming album was hugely increasing the number of visitors to the site—up to 35,000 a month, which on the back of a four-year silence and no existing promotion was encouraging. Throughout *Already*'s promotion, the website was often the only way fans could hear the singles, see the videos, and read about the band, even in countries where the record was released.

A new record from us gradually materialised from a distant hope to a tangible article and those preparations meant a sequence of events not quite forgotten but excitingly unfamiliar. The chosen singles needed to be sub-contracted out, stripped to their underwear for remixers to operate on and return surgically enhanced. Back to Martyn's studio then.

We cut the first single, "The Next Big Thing" (a defiantly optimistic choice of title, at least), on my father's birthday, which is the only thing I remember about the day—cutting sessions being as described. That same evening, Andy Ross, manager Gail, and I met EMI's head of video, Trudy, and her recommendation for director of the first video for the album, Chris Cunningham. We'd already seen Chris's showreel and loved it. He was keen to work with us because of a tenuous connection with the Aphex Twin, who once remixed a song of ours—a musician he much admired. Slight as that may seem, it was an improvement from the usual director's approach of "Well, why not?" It was a great meeting, by which I mean everyone stayed well past the thirty minutes or so they thought it would last and got very drunk, leaving only when the bar staff ordered them to.

I did my first real interview for the album, a "phoner" from Japan, done well in advance as usual for that country's press. The success we'd had in Japan was thrilling. I'd always enjoyed touring there more than most other places, liked the people, and found the interviewers unusually thought provoking. Where British and Australian press has a cynical, accusatory tone and the American press suffers from bland goodwill, the Japanese interviewers always gave the impression of having listened hard to your music and tried to provide unusual questions. While I sat in my studio at home, answering the questions and looking at the sky, I could remember a couple of years earlier, sitting in the same position, looking at the same sky, vexed and frustrated at trying to find another obstinate line for another reluctant verse, over and over.

Open Song Surgery

With the first single comes a tour to test the water, a kind of musical Expeditionary Force hoping to avoid a Dunkirk. The way I'd always written the songs and recorded them was to provide whatever the song needed. We'd worry about who got to play what live later. It was often easy deciding who'd play the drum parts from the record or who'd recreate Al's studio parts onstage, but with the amount of electronica that was an integral part of our sound, a lot of overlap occurred.

Before the first tour for each new album, I'd have to reorganise and allocate, re-sample sounds to make the studio samples compatible with the live samplers, create new sounds to mimic studio parts, invent new guitar lines, decide which, if any, parts were too much for human ability and sequence them, and generally try to ease the music from one medium to another, from studio to live performance. It was a time-consuming job and not that creative—donkey work, basically—and with tour rehearsals imminent, I spent the remainder of the month once more up to my elbows in the album's guts.

March saw my divorce finally come through. We had little to argue about, but the lawyers must have felt left out with the simplicity of our arrangements and so organised a lengthy post mortem. My wife and I had tried hard to remain friends, largely for the sake of our daughter, and we gradually accomplished that. In a gesture of defiance at the occasion, we booked a table at a Swiss restaurant in Mayfair and decided to enjoy the occasion. It nearly worked.

As we talked about the last few years, I found you can't genuinely celebrate a moment of supreme sadness. I thought of the years of success and optimism when we'd been together, the era of doubt and the years of depression and pressure as I grew away from her, uncomfortable with myself and with everyone else. I remembered the pain I'd caused her and myself and the creeping guilt of having failed my daughter.

Not much to celebrate.

7.

APRIL

What a more appropriate month to start the English mountain bike race season than one of the wettest? Thrash, thrash, thrash, little April deluge. A summer of racing bikes on off-road courses throughout the country suggests a light dust on the faces and limbs of cyclists glistening with athletic sweat under a "Phew! What a scorcher!" sky. The reality is mud-caked drowned rats in tears of frustration, kicking and swearing at immobile bikes weighing several times what they did on the start line, machines so clogged in clay and grass you could bake them and use them for motorway bridge foundations.

Winter racing was more fun, the races lower key, and the courses drier, even if frost bite was an occasional hazard. Having spent the decade adamantly denying I would ever race, the week I was offered a place on two different teams—soon after the confidence boost of discovering an ability to haul myself over 18,000-foot Tibetan passes—I thought I had little to lose and a fair bit of swag to gain. Even in the strictly amateur categories, sponsorship is freely available, ranging from a race jersey once a year to free bikes, if you're very lucky.

A cartoon mountain-biking sheep that had appeared in the pages of *Mountain Biking UK* magazine guided, in theory, the team I raced for—the Mint Sauce Race and Flowers Team. The magazine connection meant sponsorship was most forthcoming, and we accepted tyres, jerseys, watches, T-shirts, and discounts with joy. The ethic of the team, as it was explained to me, was to camp out at the race sites, drink a lot the night before the event, and not be that bothered with competition. The drinking part was easy enough, but my touring-derived addiction to hotels meant I didn't fancy weekends spent ankle deep in mud, sleeping in a leaky tent. Even Glastonbury goers restrict that to just once a year.

Where I really tripped up though was when I started to do quite well. Racing against approximately one hundred other amateur riders also in their thirties, in series split into northern and southern England, I finished my first couple of races in the top third and then moved into the top twenty. It was good to place in the top twenty again.

To my surprise, I really enjoyed racing, and I muted the wry mutterings about throwing me off the team for getting good results by being one of the few riders on a large team who had actually made all the races. I loved the riding, racing or not.

I loved it because it proved the best escape from my mind; at 30mph down a rocky bridle path, no room exists for any thoughts other than, "Go left. Miss rock. Jump rut. Don't brake. Lift wheel," and during the interminable writing and recording—days spent pondering verses, bridges, choruses, success, failure, responsibility—the mental signal jamming of thrashing about on a bike in the best scenery in Britain or America was spiritually cleansing. Racing focused this further. Not only were there the technical and physical aspects of mastering the course, but the mental stimulation of race tactics: deciphering which riders to watch; looking for signs they were flagging; figuring out where they were strong or where their weaknesses lay; whether they tired quickly on the climbs or braked too hard on the descents or faltered over the rocks and tree roots; remembering the details and nature of the course; judging the right moment to attack and keeping the lead.

Another factor of racing that improved my mental well-being was the inarguable nature of the results. Having hit records doesn't prove that much about you. Many people will still say publicly that you're crap, and it's hard to disagree rationally. Quoting sales figures is tantamount to arguing that McDonald's is the best food in the Western world because they sell the most burgers. But in local bike races, finishing regularly in the top five, sometimes winning, showed I was good at something, no quibble. After years of music press slagging and personal insults, this had become important to my self-esteem—to be good at something, no argument.

Parallels existed with playing live too, especially at bigger gigs like festivals or stadia. Two minutes before the start, the nerves are bad enough that you feel you'd rather be anywhere else. Just standing on the start line, waiting, my heart rate can be close to half its maximum. I've read the levels of adrenaline in a musician immediately before going on stage, even at just at a pub gig, could be fatal if introduced to someone sitting at a desk. Stadium levels would presumably see the corpse jogging around the building a few times and making the coffee.

In both pursuits, the start of the event brings an explosion of adrenaline you know you'll have to pay for ten minutes later. After that weakening lull, you find your feet and get on with enjoying it, still concentrating all the time. If all goes as hoped, by the finish, the sense of satisfaction and accomplishment, not to mention ego gratification, are amongst life's greatest pleasures.

I raced throughout '96, then '97—once a month earlier in the year, up to two a month by April, once a week by June, and in August, I had a period with three races in seven days. The level of fitness I gained was not very rock 'n' roll, and the perversity of that continued to please me, particularly when the people I raced with initially expected me to have to stop for a spliff and a beer at every lap. "Training" was never a problem. If I needed to get somewhere in London, I rode my bike—nearly always quicker than a car, and with ideal parking guaranteed, I'd have been an idiot not to. As would most Londoners.

My one gleefully weak concession to rock 'n' roll excess was my bike collection—five in all: three mountain bikes, one road racer, and a seven-foot-long, white-walled tyre, fire-engine red American beach cruiser, a kind of engineless low rider. That bike I bought as my "limo" in preparation for the album's promotion. Whenever that might happen.

"Icebergs ahead!"

EMI's international department offered a fresh supply of Japanese, Finnish, and Israeli interviewers for me to feast on during April, with a noticeable lack of British press. Bugger all, in fact.

Halfway through the month, we started rehearsals for our first official UK tour in four years. We were to release the first single in early May, and the tour kicked off in the first week of that month, but the label still had not mentioned any music press interviews. I assumed this was all under control, part of the plan.

The first jolt to knock the album off-course came in April. EMI moved the single's release date. They'd scheduled "The Next Big Thing" for release when Radio 1, still Britain's most influential station, staged its own Music Week and, so we were told, not amenable to adding new singles to the playlists. That even the most myopic of planners should have foreseen this shows how they had not kept the band informed with much accuracy, or truth perhaps.

The label scheduled a new release for later in May, right after the tour finished. Since the tour couldn't be moved at this late date, it became marooned in a sea of inactivity—no press, no radio play, no forceful announcement to the world that we had returned. The news on the website brought people from around the world to the gigs, but unless you looked hard in the tour dates section of the music press or were used to checking between the gardening section and car boot sale adverts of the local press in the towns we were due to visit, you'd never have found out.

"1-2-3-4-NI! STIR!"

Rehearsals. A pattern always emerged the first few days. Day one had us thinking we were the greatest band ever and hadn't lost a thing in the months of not performing. The second day we were so truly dreadful we left depressed. The third day improved just enough for us to realise just how far we had to go to sound like a band who actually got paid to do this sort of thing.

Iain would forget which keys played samples and had to relearn musical parts. Real howlers could end songs abruptly in a fit of giggles or a rebuke from me. Alan and Jerry's backing vocals could tend towards the bovine without careful herding.

I forgot lines, usually something crucial like the first of one of our biggest singles. I sometimes did this at shows too and often mumbled something I hoped would sound more like a technical error than human failure, like "Brzap cabbage dateline fling on."

Some old songs we argued about including in the set but only one we were unanimous in our dislike of—our first proper hit, "Real, Real, Real." Other songs were like old acquaintances we'd warm to again after a couple of years, some we viewed as the office colleagues we didn't really like but were obliged to be with every day. We had a honeymoon period with the newer songs in earlier rehearsals, and we could spend most of a day's session working on a couple, alternating them to find a line between forgetting the parts through repetition and forgetting them through lack of attention.

Strangely, the least of our problems was our stand-in drummer, Wiff, who'd been our drum roadie for years and had played dates with us before when Gen had taken parental leave from an American tour to be at his daughter's birth. To be fair, Wiff had put in a Herculean effort to smooth over the loss of such a pillar of strength for the band.

"What s All This Then?"

Five days a week we'd rehearse in a room with mirrors along one wall. I'd always hated that and played with my back to it, facing the rest of the band. Iain and I rode bikes in every day, but Alan and Jerry were close enough to walk—Al would stay with Jerry for a couple of months whenever we had rehearsals, promotions, or photo shoots.

One fine spring morning, neither of them showed. After about thirty minutes of feeling annoyed at their lateness, the rest of us became intrigued. I rang Jerry's number—no reply. I rang our management to see if they knew what was going on, but they expected them to be with us. Hours passed. I got a phone call from Gail. Alan and Jerry had been arrested.

On their way to rehearsal, they'd been walking past a house with a security alarm going off. At that very moment, a van full of police arrived, stopped, and searched them, finding quantities of amphetamine—speed—on each of them. They demanded to be taken to Jerry's house, which the police also searched. While Wiff, Iain, and I waited at rehearsal, CID interviewed Alan and Jerry separately in Acton Police Station.

They should have been used to the routine by that point. On a British tour years before, some of the band and crew bought large water pistols in neon colours in Birmingham and acted as a mobile liquid-assault team, operating from the windows of the van on the drive to Leeds. An omen of impending doom came when they chose the wrong bystander to squirt, and a drenched and irate off-duty inspector pulled over the van. Apart from the ignominy of having to stand in a line on the pavement and be asked, "What's wrong with you lot? You all look like something from U2!" (I've since wondered if Bono ever tried brandishing a fake weapon whilst cruising through, say, Sarajevo), we got away with it.

Once at the Leeds hotel though, gunfight at the O.K. Leisure Baths began again. Across the road at a bus stop, a squaddie saw a bunch of guys waving guns. I'm presuming he didn't tell the police they were bright orange and fluorescent green or else they might not have spent eight hours surreptitiously sealing off the city centre and putting marksmen on the roofs surrounding the hotel. We learned about it as the doors of the lifts opened, aqua-frolicking long since over and journeying to the gig.

Hands reached in, grabbed us, and threw us against the reception wall, legs spread and arms outstretched. Descriptions were matched, and police-station interrogations took place as our support band played the longest set of their career. Twice, probably. We played the gig hours late and left Leeds the next day with the warning that charges would be pressed only if we went to the papers with the story. I wonder who felt more embarrassed?

My closest brush with prison came on day one of the *Liquidizer* tour. I'd been in the studio until 2 a.m. the night before when I'd had a call from the police inquiring about the car I'd sold three months earlier. *Would I come in to help them answer a few questions?* inquired a pleasant-voiced policewoman. To return in time for the pick-up for the first gig, I had to get up at eight and cycle to Paddington Green station, admiring the twelve-foot-high steel doors inside—a courtesy for the IRA suspects interviewed there. They made me wait for an hour after the arranged time; I sat, thinking how late I'd be.

Instead of the pleasant-voiced policewoman I expected, a caricature of a rugby player emerged, looked me up and down once, and said, "Yeah, you fit the description. I know you did it. I'm arresting you for assault." Not only was this not the way I had imagined my morning going, I hadn't a clue what he was talking about. He immediately marched me upstairs to an interrogation room. I sat down, and he told me, "Now, you can confess quickly and get it over with, be out of here in two minutes, or you can spend a night in the cell and see a solicitor in the morning." It was 10 a.m. This, I later discovered, was not quite official procedure. Or even legal.

After a very unpleasant half an hour, during which I questioned whether I had actually rammed someone whilst in a car I'd sold months earlier and then punched the other driver but just had forgotten it, I signed a statement denying involvement. As I left the police station, very late for this crucial first date, I was told with a chummy smile, "I knew it wasn't you the moment I saw you."

Maybe police procedure had come under scrutiny in the intervening years, since Alan and Jerry's treatment was far better. They were told that since they were obviously not the big boys of illegal narcotics, attempts at leniency would be made. In fact, the arresting officer was so caring that when Jerry explained in the interview the speed wasn't his and he was just taking it to a friend, the officer rapidly told Jerry the difference between intent to supply and possession, which he might prefer in court should he care to backtrack a little. The police released them with charges pending, and we resumed rehearsing as normal.

The only reaction from those around the band was that a little publicity wouldn't go amiss.

"Sorry, hair in the gate. Can we do that again please?"

Chris Cunningham's video shoot was ready. I cycled to the warehouse in Kings Cross_since I knew exactly how long it would take me and didn't want to have to get up even earlier to accommodate the vagaries of London traffic in a chauffeur-driven car, courtesy of the production company. It backfired on me. Approximately forty-five minutes before our 8 a.m. call time, the IRA informed the police they had set bombs at most of London's major rail stations, including Kings Cross.

I cycled past the traffic chaos while everyone else sat in it. Some people, like our director, arrived just thirty minutes late, having paid a taxi driver £10 for what would have been a twenty-minute walk. Others arrived much later, and some of the camera equipment didn't arrive until five hours after we were due to stand in front of it. I sat in a cold warehouse from 8 a.m., waiting for something to happen. At 10 p.m., faced with either an all-night shoot or scheduling a second day, we went home.

The set's construction was tricky enough to delay shooting for another couple of hours the next morning. Chris's idea was to film us miming the song inside what looked like a giant revolving baked bean can. He had covered the inside with bright white boards and strip lighting. A remote-controlled camera moved along the length of the can on rails. I had to sing to this camera while the entire structure rotated, the camera moving in front and behind me on the rails as the can revolved 360 degrees. Fixed to the floor in different positions but equal angles apart were three steel strut-supported harnesses for the rest of the band to strap into. This meant that at any one time, at least one of them would be at an angle where the blood would rush to his head and the metal truss and harness straps would begin to cut into his skin.

Video filming takes hours, most of which is spent waiting for technical problems to be sorted out. How long can you hang upside down? All three band members looked like tomato-headed humans with musical instruments after a few seconds. Minutes passed, and complaints started. We'd barely done the fifth take when we reached *"GET ME OUT OF HERE NOW, YOU FUCKING BASTARDS!"*

The heat from the lighting in the can rose quickly and became stifling. I had great difficulty singing the song to camera, as I spent most of my time trying not to step on the strip lights. The can came apart, showering bits of wood and foam on me during the takes. The motion and disorientation from running inside a horizon-less sphere made me queasy, but at least I wasn't an exploding tomato head.

At the end of every take, Chris revolved the can so only one perspiring, swearing person was fully upside down, and I would stand with my shoulder supporting his head to try and ease the pain. We looked like Siamese twins in the Mir space station. It didn't seem like a good point to mention that at least we weren't cold—as in the photo shoots—and I had a brief, uncharitable memory of looking past Brazilian interviewer #10 of the day at the rest of the band sitting with drinks in their hands by the side of a sun-dazzled pool.

We had tolerated two hypothermic photo sessions and the most painful video we'd ever made. This had better be worth it.

Lumps in the Coffee Creamer

At the end of the month, I met Andy Ross in a Camden coffee shop. Yes, the record release delay was unfortunate but probably for the better as it was held back to improve the single's chances. He was confident that the lack of music press coverage was temporary, and he had every faith in EMI's press office. I felt the same. But with a week until the first tour date and a single to be released not long after that, where were the interviews?

8.

MAY

The Press

It's difficult to be a British musician, a creator of music, and have much respect for the press at home. Or, as this paragraph had opened in my first draft, *If you call a spade a spade, you call a British music journalist a cunt.* No doubt they were all once sweet-faced young cherubs, but whether it's that guitar or drum kit discarded in failure—a truism self-protectively derided as a cliché—or another twist of the psyche, the style of snide, cynical points scoring with colleagues through the destructive criticism of music and musicians of all levels of success that so exemplifies the British music press becomes the raison d'être.

Personal insults, libel, even printed death wishes are fair play if the result is entertaining. A cheap laugh is the goal, and envy coaches the team. Musicians shouldn't complain at this ethical quagmire because they are sometimes well paid, and everybody knows pain cannot be felt in the 40% income tax bracket. But, except for this one, generalisations don't stand up to too much scrutiny. Some music journalists are interested in music for its own sake and can provide insight that enriches our experience of music. Music journalists don't put words in your mouth after the interview (well, just the once for me). A purpose exists to it and a need, and most bands—certainly including us—benefit from it to a large extent.

However, it's very important in Britain for journalists to discover the bands and not to happen independently of them, as we did. Andy Ross's contention had always been that this was a major part in the press's disdain of us. As an ex-writer for *Sounds*, his opinion seemed valid. Success, particularly in America, is an even greater cause for trashing if you haven't been the cause célèbre of at least one of the weeklies, and the Americans who join the gang when they support an approved band become dumb Yanks when they send a disliked one into their Top 10. In eight years, we'd gone from playing every indie dive in London to selling millions of albums and had Top 10 singles on either side of the Atlantic but had only one *NME* front cover. A favoured band with one Top 40 single could get three times that every couple of months. But that, like bad reviews, is the nature of the press, and we did have many good reviews, particularly in our first couple of months.

Other factors made us—particularly me—disliked. It's fair to say I often presented the press with an unpleasant persona: argumentative, arrogant, and pompous (who was I to steal their thunder?). I always felt combative and defensive in interviews, but then, from very early on, the magazine's tone was very GCSE. "Jesus Jones are crap. Discuss." Most of all, I really didn't fit. I was obviously middle class like most musicians and journalists but refused make the requisite attempt to hide it with an assumed accent, a manner learnt by rote and the adopted thousand-yard stare to be interpreted as other worldly, gifted, and artistic. I wouldn't conform to the ironically rigid notion of rock-n-roll behavior. I could do the journalist's job, and I was doing what they had always wanted to.

Disliking a band or a record or a gig seemed fair enough, but the method of communicating that sometimes didn't. The "angle" wouldn't allow actuality to interfere, and so the press would remove negatives from interview transcriptions to prove a point against us; journalists would overlook artwork details to show how unpleasant I was; interviewers would make hilariously obvious contradictions about a single to illustrate its worthlessness.

Occasional good reviews surprised me but unfortunately left no other impression, and from the summer of '89 onwards, I felt as if an army of pygmies trailed me and shot darts at me. You sing in a band partly because you want people to like you, and you end up with foaming-mouthed harpies wishing you dead—your idiotic naivety can be depressing.

Above the regular criticism, two incidents really stand out.

NME reviewed us at Reading Festival in 1989, giving us one of the first real savagings. I remember little mention of the music. When Andy Ross wrote a letter to the magazine questioning the reviewer's ability to judge a band from thirty-five miles—where she'd been when we were onstage—the letters page editor had allowed her to respond since Andy had been a music journalist and knew the way the system worked and should know better than to complain.

The second incident was well beyond a bad review. At the start of 1993, our agent had told us one of the organisers of Glastonbury Festival had a sponsorship meeting with Steve Sutherland, an interesting character who had previously mounted an anti-*NME* campaign, culminating in calling it "dogshit" shortly before accepting a better paid job there. Reputedly, Sutherland had said the *NME*'s sponsorship of Glastonbury—using *IPC Magazine*'s money—was dependent on Jesus Jones not appearing on the festival bill. Gail sent an indignant letter to the magazine's editor, Alan Jones, asking if this was official magazine policy and received a mealy-mouthed reply that neither confirmed nor denied. To the chagrin of EMI and Food, I refused to have anything to do with the paper thereafter—no interviews, quotes, or free tickets. However desperate we became, I didn't want to have to deal with people like that.

"Shut up, go away, die!"

With such a lowly status in the press, we weren't expecting much from the papers. Andy Ross and I had discussed how bad it would be before I'd written a note for the album, a similar conversation to the one I'd had with several music industry people before they'd heard any of the new songs. In May, what I didn't know, was EMI's press office frantically tried to get us press, anything at all. And the media refused. When asked to interview the band, they got a flat-out "No" or "We'll see" ("No" for the gutless).

At a point in time much further along in the process than normal for the record-releasing business, I had yet to do a single national music-press interview for *Already*, and I honestly didn't think the chances would improve. As the music press had become less and less interesting because of, or possibly resulting in, the death of rock as a potent form of musical rebellion, originality, and the unconventional, its power had increased within the music industry, like a kind of Chinese government of music—former radicals assuming tyrannical authority. It also acted as a career springboard into British radio—including the all-important Radio 1—and had a larger effect on the playlists than it ever did before. For us, it had meant an almost total blockade—no interviews, no play listing.

We got a few isolated plays on Radio 1 for this single but none for the next, and nearly no public awareness that we had returned. I wasn't being told this as rehearsals started, but that was probably best for our morale. Unbeknown to us, a few weeks before the first single's release, it was all over. The album was stillborn, we'd had it. It had been decided.

My tour diary, written in the van every day, gives an insight into the way we felt at the time. What we didn't know then was that this small, unglamorous tour would be the only trip we would do that year—a long, dismal way from the days of nine months a year spent on the road, around the world.

Day 1 - Thursday May 8: The Next Big Disaster

Some start. Straight back from the final rehearsal which went as badly as final rehearsals always do and Gail rings me with the news that the label has delayed the single for yet another week. Also, it's sounding like the American EMI's approach to the release plan for *Already* is "I dunno, what do you think?"

In the van to Jerry's, I find the promotion has, in fact, begun with a real slagging of the single in *Melody Maker*, starting off as they mean to continue, no doubt. Two minutes later, tour manager/drummer Wiff arrives in a van he had just crashed into the back of a truck. Then it starts to rain.

It's Thursday for the rest of England, but Liverpool seems to exist in a perennial Sunday. With this many boarded-up shops, surely only chipboard sales are booming here.

Soundcheck is nerve-wracking with lots of horrendous mistakes, including me botching the intro to "Wishing It Away." If I do that in the set, we'd have to start the song all over again, and while the intro's good, I could definitely wait until the next night to play it again. We get to meet Grant, our lighting man, for the first time, and Justin gets his first attempt at doing our sound in about seven years. We play about twenty minutes worth of songs to try and outmanoeuvre the Beast of Big Mistake, which is lurking malevolently behind the amps somewhere.

After eating curry up the road from the venue, we return to the hotel to sit and wait in a state of marginal anxiety in which you'll watch whatever is on TV if it doesn't last more than about three minutes. We're due on stage at 10:45 p.m., so we leave the hotel at ten o'clock for me to get half an hour's warm up before we play.

In the dressing room, I play guitar and sing mostly our songs but also fragments I remember or noodle from The Beatles and Eels songs. The rest of the band pace around the room, talking rubbish and halfheartedly warm up. I put down the guitar and talk rubbish with them for the last ten minutes.

It's strange walking on stage. People are cheering, but the atmosphere feels muted, as though I'm overcompensating for the nerves earlier (I'm not nervous at all. Although, with a small not-sold-out venue, there's not that much to be nervous about). The first half of the set just feels a little polite. We get to the older stuff and loosen up a bit. Our equipment shares this sense of abandon as it begins to take unscheduled breaks, and Alan, Jerry, and I each get our turn to appreciate what Jesus Jones would sound like without our guitars. "Guitar Tech" Phil gets a couple of tours worth of breakdowns in thirty minutes, but it serves him right for being nonchalant.

We head to the dressing room soaked in sweat, talking the usual post-gig, hyped-up rubbish, mostly about how great we are and "did you hear me when …" After an hour of alcohol/juice/water/food, autographs, and nattering, we return to the strange Euro-cubicle hotel rooms for further celebration and/or too little sleep—great childlike self-indulgence.

Day 2 - Friday May 9: Manic & Misery

I go for a run around the docks first thing, which is okay for the exercise and vista, but as an activity, jogging is deeply unpleasant, and in my experience is best left for life-threatening or preserving occasions. However, the mountain-bike race season waits for no debilitating tour schedule, and so I'm plodding like a dweeb around the docks, thus setting myself up for a day of tortuous muscle pain.

We leave Liverpool en route for Newcastle at ten in the morning with Phil's eccentric driving to keep us entertained. We overshoot the A1 turn off, nearly mow down a pedestrian on a zebra crossing, brake late for everything, occasionally swerve to the left, and spend ten minutes at teeth rattlingly high revs until Phil remembers the van has a fifth gear. For lunch, we entertain Iain's romantic notion of finding fine pub food, which inevitably turns out to be microwaved, instant sauce mush. Exactly the sort of food that gives England the culinary reputation as the place where they boil pizza.

A radio interview and then a short drive to the Riverside— a venue we played years ago—punctuates an afternoon of waiting for me. The sound is great onstage, as long as the PA isn't turned on. If the audience are to hear anything, the band gets swamped with a full sound-spectrum roar that obliterates any nuances, like musical keys. The bass is particularly bad, making the stage rumble but not providing anything for the singers to pitch to. Not perhaps ideal.

I can never figure out how such a disparity exists between how well the band thinks the gig goes and how good the audience thinks it went. We have a crap one tonight—less technical problems but, as suspected, the onstage sound is diabolical. A loud nonstop bass rumble continues through the songs and the breaks. Why the local monitor crew does nothing about it defies logic, since even deafness couldn't prevent an awareness of the bone-shaking noise.

I'm suffering a sore throat that hasn't changed in about three weeks, and maybe it's that or the string of late nights, but my voice is not in good shape and needs careful guiding through a tough set. But, by the end of the set, my voice is returning, and we've stopped bothering about our music sounding like a plane crash.

Backstage, after the show, our agent has a few words of wisdom that will change the set in the future. He and his girlfriend really enjoyed the gig, as did a string of people who proceed throughout the damp and smoky dressing room, issuing forth from the standard filthy, sagging sofas.

Day 3 - Saturday May 10: Sheffield, The Glamour of the North

More motorway madness as Phil hits the Red Bull early in our rocket van south to Sheffield and the Leadmill, another venue from our past. Today is a landmark for me as it marks the 17th anniversary of the first gig Gen and I ever played. Gen's currently in Japan with his wife and soon-arriving daughter, and I'm tapping away on a Powerbook as northern England goes past the window at 100 mph. We didn't imagine this back then.

Just outside Sheffield, the rain starts. Rain doesn't do much for most cities, and Sheffield, with its vast empire of concrete, gets a real visual drubbing—a good day for staying in the dressing room once we get to the gig.

I eat in the venue, watching the support band, the Peccadilloes, do their soundcheck. I like their single, "U.S.S.O," and I'm looking forward to their set. Probably more than them, as they go on to what looks like about twenty people in a venue which holds many multiples of that. They are good, but it must seem pretty pointless to them as they finish to virtually no applause from an embarrassed audience.

By the time we go on, the venue has filled out, not full by a long way but definitely looking healthy. The onstage sound is good, and my guitar sounds just right. We play well, despite the occurrence of the inevitable horror-mistake—the start of "Wishing It Away" gets screwed up, and we have to do it again. Well, I always liked that bit.

Off stage, I'm feeling pretty contemplative again. This isn't the great return we had planned on. The crucial problem is that EMI, by delaying the single's release date three weeks, have scuppered the promotion for the tour. Radio stations won't be playing the single this far in advance—almost a month, for these first few dates—and so, to a large extent, we're preaching to the converted.

In the van on the way home, I type a fax to Food, not really achieving anything but venting my frustration at how the band have spent years on this record, much energy and preparation with the website and rehearsals, and yet, we're on the least-promoted tour we've ever done in this country (bar the last "secret" one). Not a cheering thought at 4:30 a.m. as I get into my bed at home in London.

Day 4 – Monday May 12:
Working in Wales

Phil negotiates his terrifying way to the M4, heading for Wales and tonight's gig at the University of Glamorgan. The student bar below the venue has some of the worst food known to man, and Iain suffers badly after it for days. Given that his intestines appear to be wildly out of control normally, this is horrifying. The bar does, however, have the Time Crisis arcade game, which involves shooting people a lot and is just dandy by me. And they have "The Next Big Thing" on the jukebox, which explains why that song goes down better tonight than any other.

The gig is great. Lots of people crowd surf and yelling unintelligibly, lots of work for the bouncers to do. For the band, the lighting is too dark, and as I'm dressed entirely in black, Alan has difficulty seeing me, which explains the perilous swings of his guitar near my head and some of the strange chord changes throughout the set. We keep changing the set to try to get the best version, but we boob tonight by playing "For a Moment" as the encore. After the album comes out, this'll be a good idea I'm sure but not now.

The backstage scene after the show is chaotic, the band standing about in various stages of dress, still dripping sweat, while a stream of mostly uninvited people drift in. Sometimes this is good, sometimes this is bad, but I got the impression there wasn't much to do but drink and drug yourself to babbling incoherence in the semi-wilds of Glamorgan.

Day 5 – Tuesday May 13: Roof Coffee at Last

With Bath being close to Wales and Alan and I having relatives in the area, we'd driven there after the gig. I woke up at my dad's house and went for another ill-advised run. The scenery alongside the Kennet and Avon canal and the Avon river was great, but every fool dog owner and their shit-pumping, slobbering, out-of-control animal impeding my sweaty progress made the exercise itself even more unpleasant. Ill temper versus distemper.

At the venue, Alan does an interview with a bass magazine, and I get the guitarists' version. It's then time for more student cafe food, served incredibly slowly—this is really only notable because if I eat too close to the gig, the breathing and exertion of singing makes it quite likely I'll witness dinner in reverse.

The gig is even better than last night and twice as hot. Phil is threatening legal action if he has to continue to handle guitars with this much corrosive sweat on them. During the last song, "Idiot Stare," I notice whenever I fling an arm in the air, an arc of sweat droplets follow it. That'll be nice for the front row.

The after show was chaos, as any after show with a lot of friends and relatives always is—a string of high-speed, brief conversations spread over a couple of hours. But what is really irking me is someone has nicked my post-gig Red Bull. Doh!

Day 6 – Wednesday May 14: Still Not Sure What Tense to Write In

Hull doesn't seem to have much going for it. It's a sunny day when we arrive, and the city looks ugly. This is the equivalent of putting on your best clothes and still looking a mess. After a riotous radio interview—about five people in the control room, all simultaneously asking questions—I try and do some shopping. At 5:25 p.m. in Hull, that was a little optimistic, as some sort of Yorkshire siesta/early closing is in operation. Instead, I wander to the gig for soundcheck and a couple of interviews. We play AC/DC's "Gone Shootin'" for the last soundcheck song. Probably just as well they didn't book a support band tonight.

The hotel is hilarious, what's left of it. It's hard to tell if it's being built up or pulled down. Lots of references to Beirut ensue as we trip over electricity cables, cement bags, and tools, traipsing through the debris to the rooms.

We'd been anxious about how this gig would go, having never played here before and in the light of the first couple northern gigs, but we get to the gig to find it packed out. The first good sign. The second good sign was that the onstage sound, which is always totally different during the gig than at soundcheck, sounded superb.

Having played enough gigs now to no longer be making stupid mistakes, we combine our good fortune to have a belter of a gig. Okay, so we're still having some problems with backing vocals, but otherwise, the gig is a joyous combination of good playing and enthusiasm in front of a great crowd. "The Next Big Thing" had received a tiny amount of airplay, at least locally, and the difference in its response is noticeable. Another reason to be cheerful.

The heat is incredible. By the third song, I'm sweating heavily, and by the end, I feel as dehydrated as I'd expect to in a summer mountain bike race. The lack of oxygen starts to make singing hard, and "Idiot Stare" doesn't have the long notes live that it has on record as a result.

The only negative part of the evening is someone has again nicked my post-gig Red Bull. I inform the crew this is now a sackable offense.

Day 8 - Friday May 16:
Routine Sweating

Nottingham traffic, motorway madness, motorway traffic, dreary English towns, open countryside, and then, three hours later, Middlesborough. Now, I'm sorry if you live here, but this place is where inhabitants of truly ugly cities come to feel better about their hometowns—flat, grey, and hardly a building over two storeys. Strange, also, how all the men sport that military/convict hairstyle with added moustache. And everyone is in a track suit.

Routine. It's all settled now—emails and diary for me in the van on the way from city to city, more of that at the hotel, and from there to the soundcheck, sometimes via an interview. We usually play "Zeroes and Ones," "Wishing It Away," "The Next Big Thing," and "International Bright Young Thing" at soundcheck, those songs using the range of technology we have with us, as well as the full array of backing vocals. Then to the hotel.

The gig is good, not great. We have a great crowd, but it doesn't seem like anyone has done any promotion here. "The Next Big Thing" gets virtually no recognition, and as it is the third new song in a row, the early part of the set falls a bit flat. My voice is okay, despite this being the fifth night in a row and a late one at that, but I go through a period of playing badly and being distracted by what the rest of the band are doing. It's always how you play that really determines how much you enjoy a gig, so thankfully, I get better by the end of the set, coinciding with a spate of old songs that are what this crowd are really here for.

It's another sweaty gig. When I come off stage, I wring streams of sweat from my shirt.

"Absolutely world fucking class!"

The last three dates of the diary didn't get written, as we got closer to home and the free time that touring provides diminished. We'd played a great gig in Norwich with a band called A on the Football Association's cup final day, and I got a lift home with a friend in order to wake up a few hours later and ride a bike race. Two days later, we played another stormer in Exeter at a tiny venue called the Cavern. The venue's size, the crowd's reaction, and our enthusiasm made it reminiscent of gigs in our very early days. A run of good gigs made us nervous about the last one, the 100 Club in London.

In addition to friends and family and most of the people who worked with us being there, press and record companies from around the world were present too, and the American EMI had brought some big industry names from press and television. That sort of pressure usually counted against us, but on that night, we really pulled it off. The confidence and ability had returned, and a superb crowd packed the venue. Nothing malfunctioned seriously, no-one screwed up badly, and it felt good to play these songs so well. It was one of those gigs that actually was the way I'd always imagined being in a band would be like.

In the tiny dressing room at the back of the club, Dave Balfe, who still advised us despite having left Food years earlier, stormed in and gushed, "Brilliant! Absolutely world fucking class! It's just a pity you're not a new band."

Adding to that insight, he asked me how the radio play was going. The glare Gail threw at him let me know just how little bad news they were telling us.

I spent the last week of May fending off the anticlimax of finishing the tour with days of promotion—nearly all international press and radio and a couple of hours spent hanging around MTV for two brief interviews. Al was with me, and he spent the time drinking beer and joining in with my critiquing the bands shown on the TV. No-one from the record company attended, and the interviewers were busy elsewhere, apart from the ten minutes spent briefly quizzing us.

Afterwards, we sat in the sunshine outside the MTV canteen, next to the Regents Canal in Camden. The single would be released in a few days, but we felt no sense of urgency, no sense of occasion, none of the nervous excitement we'd had in the build up to every other release.

We had a good idea of what was about to happen.

9.

JUNE

The Next Big Thing

Monday, June 2, 1997, the release date for our 11th UK single, "The Next Big Thing." After a long gap (like four years and four months), it's a rule with few exceptions that if the first single doesn't succeed, the subsequent singles and album are write-offs. All the favours are called in for this first release. Friends in TV and radio and press get the reminders of that little bit extra the band did for them last time around. Every scrap of promotion you do is used to fuel the return drive into the spotlight. Once all your Get Out of Jail Free cards are gone, you're on your own. Either your rejuvenated success fills the tank, sending you cruising back into the public eye with the follow-up singles, or you're on the hard shoulder without a breakdown recovery card. We already felt like hitchhikers.

In the years between *Perverse* and this release, I'd often contemplated what I'd do if the album bombed. The amount of money EMI was contractually obliged to advance us if they wanted another album meant anything less than good sales of *Already* would guarantee us being dropped. Although I could really see myself as a bicycle courier, and as the band's sole writer, it would be a while before I needed to run red lights while screaming at taxi drivers (I did it anyway, just for the practice). Of course I wanted to keep making music for as long as possible since I still loved doing that, despite the last three years, and besides, who'd really want to swap this lifestyle for one with designated hours, less international travel, and no-one occasionally sending you their sexy underwear?

Becoming a producer was out of the question. I'd already done some of that, and, in comparison with the likes of Martyn and *Perverse*'s producer, Warne Livesey, it was obvious to me I didn't have the ability. In the music industry, that doesn't have to be a consideration, but I fancied both paying the bills and living with my conscience. I could revert to being just a guitarist, hide away in another band, and let someone else answer "So, how did you guys get the name?" but I came to realise at some point I'd enjoy singing as much as playing guitar. Also, I doubted the domineering side of my personality would lie dormant while following someone else's orders.

The website design I was doing in partnership was fun and something I could see leading somewhere. Most of all though, Jesus Jones still had plenty of life left around the world as far as we were concerned, and while places we could still play existed, I was determined to push it as far as it would go.

And why shouldn't we make a comeback? Others had pulled it off. Texas had emerged around the same time as us and returned stronger in '97. James did okay with a new single after a long gap. So the Stone Roses return didn't go the way they had hoped, but at least they went down in flames, which is better than just stalling with engine failure.

Death Threat of My Own

The "midweek" came in—the estimation of the singles' chart position based on comparative sales of all the other records on release. The remote notion it might all be over had suddenly become the icy realisation that we were in real trouble, and the easy life was about to change. We didn't stand a chance of entering the Top 40 unless we suddenly got national-radio airplay, which was unlikely without some sort of major publicity coup, like me assassinating a head of state. Even then, the likes of the presidents of Mali or Tajikstan wouldn't suffice—it was either a bullet for Helmut Kohl or a bomb for the single.

Call me a woolly liberal if you will, but I preferred more artistic than political statements, so we started rehearsals for a gig in Amsterdam at the end of the week; we'd avoid hearing the chart position by driving across Belgium on Sunday afternoon.

The Last Night Stand

We didn't ask for an explanation why this single had been received better than any of our others in Belgium and Holland. We were on radio playlists there, and if the record company wanted to fly us to Brussels for all the food and drink we could handle, so much the better. Okay, so they wanted two of us to talk to the press for a few hours. We still got the infinitely better end of the deal as far as I was concerned. Plus, being slagged off in French isn't so bad, especially if you don't speak it well. Conscious of the single's plight back home, it was time to relish these opportunities and live it up. To be wined and dined by the record company after the interviews would be so much more piquant with the knowledge it was unlikely we'd return again soon.

Afterwards, a limousine drove me and Al from Brussels to Amsterdam while we argued drunkenly all the way about whether team sports were any good or not (Me: No, Al: Yes). For us, it just passed the time, but we were lucky the driver didn't beat the crap out of us, even if we weren't arguing in Flemish.

At the mini-festival in Amsterdam, we were "the old band," according to the Dutch journalist interviewing me beforehand. I told him kids didn't say things like that in my day. They had more respect back then. The Supernaturals—a band also on Food and with a great album out—were on before us, their career just entering the exciting phase back home: having hits, venturing abroad, comparing McDonald's menus (and you thought John Travolta in *Pulp Fiction* was the first), and having burly truckers on the channel ferry threatening them. As far as we knew, we were probably going to Japan, and, of course, we'd be returning to America, so there'd be plenty more gigs abroad for us.

After that show, we did not play another gig in what should have been the *Already* tour cycle. I'm pleased, then, that it was a bloody good one. It wasn't an easy crowd. They were more interested in staying late because they'd paid the money and were too drunk to walk out than they were in seeing another band, but we went down well, surprising the journalists, hopefully with our youthful vigour as well as the odd tune. A week later, we received a glowing report from the record company, saying the radio station that transmitted the show live had loved it, and overall, the promotion and gig had been a great success. They got some value for their giant restaurant bill then.

Sure enough, the next day we gorged Belgian chocolate en route to Calais when Gail got the call about the single's chart position. Once, six years previously, she'd rung me as soon as she'd heard to congratulate us on entering the album charts at number one. This time, it took a couple days before she even broached the subject. I was too despondent to ask. I can't now remember the exact position—sticklers for details will have to remain irritated that I'm not bothered about finding it out—but it entered somewhere in the fifties and was, therefore, our worst chart entry ever. And it didn't improve.

Still, at least we had America, and the record company there had begun to formulate an encouraging plan.

Another Slight Hitch

In June 1997, 180-odd EMI employees in the US awoke one morning to read in the newspapers that they no longer had jobs. One of the big six, multinational record companies had shut down, an almost unthinkable event. It's a rare decade that sees that. Weren't we the lucky ones? The two subsidiary labels would fight over the biggest-selling artists. The rest of the bands could either stay on the Titanic by being band number eighty-one on an overcrowded sister label that hadn't originally signed them or take to the lifeboats once contractual permission was given—that was our decision.

Getting a new label in America didn't prove hard, but sorting the details, the contracts, and the plans turned into an arcane process that would take well over six months. As I write, Combustion Records will release *Already* within a few weeks, but as far as 1997 goes, America went from being the country of our greatest success and a place we still had high hopes for to being completely out of the picture. No doubt luck had helped us with our early success there, but we were clearly overdrawn at Good Fortune Bank Ltd. six years later.

I don't suppose those 180-odd people were too happy either.

Round 2

Back at home, the schedule for the album fell apart with the single's failure. Food hastily delayed its release date until August in the hope the second single might ride in on a pure-white steed and save the day—an appropriate fantasy metaphor. Of course, while really only a slim chance existed, it was better than not trying at all. The last-minute change of plan meant review copies of the album had already gone to the press almost two months before it would be available in shops, cocking up that part of the promotion even further. Not that the press held many surprises (you'll be incredulous to find out). Although it was interesting to see how the approach and ideas I'd had about music that had kickstarted Jesus Jones in 1988 became very fashionable almost a decade later. Certainly, the press for the lauded U2 album released that summer, *Pop*, often featured references to us, even if it seemed we were only responsible for the worst parts of that style. One magazine gave *Pop* three-out-of-five stars and referred to us by replacing the vowels in the band's name with asterisks, as you would a swear word. Pages later, *Already* was reviewed as "The new U2 album but with better songs" for which, intriguingly, we got only two stars. Not song fans, I took it.

Preparations to make "Chemical #1" the next single got underway. Food pulled out all the stops and got some great remixers to work on the song, amongst the best we'd had. Also above normal were the video treatments, about nine in total. Food suggested shoots in a warehouse in Reading (IRA bombs unlikely there), in and around a house in Brighton, and one that would require eight days in Namibia. Now, you know where this book is going, and I had a good idea then too. Damn right we were off for a week in Africa!

In the meantime, EMI had requested, with meaningful glances, we record a song from their catalogue for a centenary-celebration album they were planning. I chose that teenage favourite of mine, The Stranglers' "Go Buddy Go," above Kate Bush's "Wuthering Heights" and "Sugar, Sugar" by The Archies and rewrote it in preparation for a recording session a few days before the Namibia shoot.

The Height of Summer

That summer was miserable, wet, and cold. I raced at least once a week now, mostly in a small series in East London—that well-known mountain biking mecca—and remember shivering on the start line for most of the races there. I raced in Brighton on my thirty-third birthday, the day after the summer solstice. It rained like it has no right to in a country without a tropical rainforest. When I could no longer even push my bike through the clay, I gave up. It was my birthday. I wanted a bike race, not an Army selection course.

On the last night of June, I went to see Gen's new band, Baby Chaos. They, too, had difficulties with their American label. Although theirs had the decency to not collapse entirely. They kept being promised all manner of exciting prospects that always had a good reason for never materialising. Watching them do a great show but knowing the behind-the-scenes tribulations made me see the parallels and the arbitrary nature of the music industry and of fashion.

Or maybe Gen and I just shared that account at Good Fortune Bank Ltd.

10.

July

The best that can be said about the recording of our version of "Go Buddy Go" was that my Hugh Cornwall impression gave us all a good laugh. Not quite all, since it wasn't worth Alan flying over for the sake of one bass line, and so, I played bass, making it two impressions of the members of The Stranglers—half the band, not bad! Otherwise, the lack of a sense of occasion and the summer of 1997's standard-issue grey sky made for a perfunctory session. However, we finished in time for me to ride across London for one last race before the flight to Namibia.

Future Publishing had asked me to write a piece on the filming of the "Chemical #1" video, and the excerpt is worth including here, even if it's just to show how we danced while Rome burned.

Chemical #1 in Namibia

The gun was much heavier than I'd expected. I could see the grooved surface of the percussion cap behind the cocked hammer, and the flat explosion, as it detonated, kicking the gun hard upwards, dulled my hearing momentarily. The 9mm bullet kicked up a flume of rock and dust a couple of inches away from the pipe I'd been aiming for, and at about seventy metres, that was okay by me.

"Good!" said the Afrikaans policeman. "Now would you like to use the grenade launcher?"

Well, why not?

We'd flown overnight to Windhoek, Namibia's capital, hired VW "Combi" vans, and driven the four hundred kilometres to Swakopmund and the Atlantic Ocean, twelve hundred kilometres northwest of Cape Town. To call the place a seaside resort, whilst accurate, would be misleading—this is hardly Benidorm. For a start, it's tiny. Then the problem with the location: from Windhoek, we'd travelled west over rolling hills and grassland—the typical southern African bushveld: the nearer we got to the coast, the less the vegetation—until one hundred kilometres from Swakopmund, the Namib desert swept in: flat, arid, treeless, grassless, gravel flats, barren, brown, isolated inselberg mountains, and at the end of the journey, sand dunes rising to over ninety metres high. Then Swakopmund, besieged by sand and sea—more of a village than a town—sitting (as linguists will have already ascertained) by the mouth of the Swakop river—a waterway which only sees surface water once every few years, and even then, only as a flash flood. Quite why the German settlers of the last century chose to live here is puzzling. That they decided to recreate a Bavarian village in this desolate place is a joyous testament to European colonial's more extreme idiosyncrasies. Here we are then, Swakopmund—Hansel and Gretel, meet Lawrence of Arabia.

Back to the weaponry. Our location scout had suggested a long-deserted copper mining village fifty kilometres into the desert. Getting there involved traversing a series of increasingly tricky gravel and sand roads culminating in a Closed sign before a heavily corrugated, boulder-strewn "road" leading to the site.

After a journey like that, we didn't really want to see the location fuzzing with Namibia's blue-uniformed paramilitary police.

Presumably bored of their training manoeuvres in the desert and with the subordinate ranks (the black Namibians) off marching for days on end in the sand and heat, the officers (the white Namibians) were more than willing to help us shoot up their country. "Would you like some smoke bombs for this shot? Oh, go on then! Would an explosion in the background look good? I think we could fit that in. Have you ever used a handgun before? A grenade launcher?" It didn't seem like it would be long before we'd be driving tanks into Swakopmund and firing a few shells down Karl-Liebknecht-Straße as our cheery moustachioed kommandos looked on amiably.

So, we stand around like goofy popstars miming our silly song as these ex-members of the South African Defence Force, the army that fought Namibia's brutal war of independence on the side of apartheid and colonialism, stare at us through their sunglasses.

The next shot involves me driving the Land Rover that contains the band and the sporting paraphernalia relevant to the video—mountain bikes and snow boards—"as fast as you can." We wait twenty minutes while the police clear away their booby traps from the area where the camera crew want to film from.

More filming, more driving. Meanwhile, the police are getting bored. We're not using enough firepower, and their honeymoon period with us is wearing off.

Two of our local crew are talking a short distance down the hill from the camera crew and the police. One of the men in blue asks us if they are foreigners or locals, presumably because the police assassination of dead locals causes less of an international incident. A shot gets fired at them, a few feet to their left. Then another, to the right. Possibly under the impression that if they ignore the bullets, they'll go away. Neither of the crew reacts, which proves to be a mistake as the next round passes about twelve inches from one of the guys' head. It's time to leave.

As the Swakop river forges through the Namib near the end of its desert sojourn, it forms a stunning canyon vista, a massive array of dark fissures in the earth that stretch for miles into the distance, overlooked sternly by the Rossing mountains. This vast, desolate area is appropriately known as Moon Valley. Although the moon has perhaps more vegetation and definitely more water. This is the location for the mountain biking filming, the bit I'm really looking forward to.

However, this is a video shoot, and the budget didn't run to hiring a helicopter, Tour de France-style, to trail my progress through a forty-mile stretch of wilderness. Instead, we get to ride up and down the steep gullies that make their eventual way to the river, cruising the flat crests of the watersheds, and dropping down the loose rock and sand inclines.

It should be explained here that the demarcation lines within the band are roughly that I do the energetic and hard-work parts, and the other three handle the more archetypal rock-n-roll aspects. They were the first people to eagerly misinterpret the title, "Chemical #1."

In a performance later described as "shit" by one of the camera crew, Jerry quickly finds his nerve to be in the same condition as his cardiovascular system and opts to spectate rather than lie panting in the dust with a collapsed Kona on top of him and sand sticking to his profusely sweating face. Alan, whose body has taken this opportunity to remind him of all those late nights and all that vodka, is faring better but facing a crisis of ambition over ability—his were by far the best crashes. Iain, however, has grabbed the bull by the horns, or so it must feel, as he plummets swiftly down a trail-less gravel precipice, following my back wheel and the director's exhortation to take the steepest, most difficult route from top to bottom.

We do take after take, sitting so far off the back of the bikes for balance that our chests rest against the back of the saddles, trying to avoid the back brake locking up and sliding the bike out of control, trying to avoid the front brake (A.K.A. "the ejector lever") altogether. At the end of an impressively audacious novice performance, Iain comments, "Fear isn't normally something I associate with being on a bike." The penny drops—Chemical #1, indeed.

All through that night, the wind punches the hotel windows and scythes through the palm trees lining the beach outside, bending their fronds to ninety degrees—don't try this at home. Perhaps it's me. My visit to Lanzarote, just off the Saharan coast where "a couple inches of rain a year is unusual," was a wash out. A long, freak storm in Mediterranean Minorca made an optimistic biking holiday there as muddy as a week in the Lake District. And one of my two trips to Australia coincided with floods in New South Wales the size of Western Europe. What my freak-weather blighted existence is experiencing this time is the worst sandstorm in Namibia for seven years.

My first inkling that all is not well is at the wakeup time of 5:30 a.m. when I stumble groggily into the bathroom and discover a quarter of an inch of sand covering every surface and a fine, sparkling mist of the stuff descending from the skylight. Sand is in my toothbrush, in the soap, in my clothes, in my razor, and even horrifyingly, on the toilet paper—it's the ultimate beach picnic nightmare.

The local crew are refusing to come out, as they like the paintwork on their cars the way it is. Later in the week, I see a car that has been in the sandstorm. The front of the bonnet is beautifully smoothed of all paint so the bare metal fades in towards the front of the car, and the headlights have the appearance of an old piece of glass on the beach.

At eight o' clock, tired of waiting on "maybe later," I leave to do some shopping. Sand and wind are obliterating the town. I feel like I've wandered into a documentary about natural disasters. Eerily, visibility is at about one hundred feet with the sun just visible, looking more lunar than solar. Small drifts, parodies of the dunes a few hundred yards away, are ganging up at every street corner and snaking across the roads. It's soon apparent why the streets are empty as the wind blows sand into my eyes, ears, nose, and mouth and stings any skin it comes into contact with—all this for a tube of toothpaste.

Returning to the hotel, I find evidence of eccentric Namibian service. The bed is perfectly made, the room is tidied, the welcome chocolate mint is on the pillow, and the welcome half inch of sand is all over the toilet. Still, several local farmhouses have had their roofs removed in the storm, so I expect they have sand in the bathroom too.

By 10 a.m., Director Stuart, driven by remorseless artistic frenzy and the knowledge that all the equipment here is hired, decides to brave the elements, and so we drive into the dying storm to film a few shots of us standing about, trying to look cool and iconic whilst being skinned alive. I feel like a butcher's shop carcass wearing sunglasses.

The storm is done by early afternoon, and our convoy of vans and Land Rover heads into the sand dune belt that runs parallel to the coast between Swakopmund and Walvis Bay. Some of the dunes here are big enough to be permanent landmarks, and the Matterhorn, at around ninety metres—although far smaller than some of the dunes a few hundred kilometres to the south—juts impressively into the cloudless sky.

The first shot here involves climbing over the other side of the Matterhorn to where the uninterrupted view is of a sea of dunes below us stretching magically to the Atlantic. It's a phenomenal sight, enriched in a sort of stoic way by having to plod half a mile uphill over sand with all the film and sound equipment. Okay, so I personally didn't have to do that, but dressed for the shoot in a woolen jersey, combat trousers, and snowboarding boots, I figured my suffering was at least a token attempt at sympathy with the sand Sherpas of the crew.

It took two hours to climb the dune and set the shot up. By this time, the fading light that would be gone by 5:30 introduced a note of anxiety as the crew coordinated the last few details over walkie talkies. And, with impeccable timing, here, somewhere to the left of the middle of nowhere, come a large group of tourists. Stuart gawps in mute disbelief as, clad in canoe helmets and holding small sheets of chipboard, they stride to the top of the dune and into shot. Then, a woman whose strident Californian accent scathes the dunes like the storm earlier in the day instructs them as one by one they lie on their chipboard toboggans and drop down the dune face first, leaving great trails in the previously unblemished sand for the unforgiving attention of our camera. One of them starts singing the chorus of a six-year-old hit of ours. I grit my teeth and discover more hidden sand. And an English voice yells in despair, "Fucking TWATS!"

Luckily, the budget had room for postproduction trickery then.

The next day, the Matterhorn was ours alone, and we would shoot the sand boarding scenes. Alan, with novice's naiveté, discovered the best approach: point the board straight down and go like hell, thus leaving you to fall off at high speed on the bottom of the slope where the sand is packed hardest. Standing at the summit of the Matterhorn, much of Namibia below you, the stiff wind blowing sand into your sweat, and a very, very steep slope falling downward to the seemingly dinky toy-sized convoy below, it took some commitment to launch yourself strapped to a chunk of wood. But, by the time we'd struggled for fifteen minutes in thirty-five-degree heat up steep sand, there was little else for it. The sweat involved in the climb and the frequent falls on the way down made for some particularly unphotogenic material. Best image from this session was of Alan, whose bald, shaven head at the top had, infomercial style, transformed into a sandy wig at the bottom.

I managed five runs—fifteen minutes uphill and fifteen seconds down each—before being called away for lip-synching shots, which saved my Achilles tendons from permanent damage.

A shot on our last day of filming called for me to drive the Land Rover through a shanty town situated, unfeasibly, sixty desert kilometres from anything human, next to what would have been a river if it contained any water. The local Topnaars, part of the Nama tribes—one of the oldest native Namibian peoples—turned out in force to laugh at the circus come to town. Physically, they're quite different from other Africans, having pale, almost yellow skin, heart-shaped faces, and a language that must be heard to be believed. It's odd enough that it includes "!" as part of its alphabet, loosely represented by the sound you get from clicking your tongue from the roof of your mouth. The conversation around us popped and clicked, little verbal firecrackers exploding in the streams of otherwise familiar human speech as I thrashed the Land Rover through the village and almost, but not quite, over the village chickens.

Then the last shot, the last obstruction before our time here is all our own for the last couple of days. Stuart has decided I perform better having worked up a sweat and so instructs me to run up the road from Swakopmund, into the desert, while the camera crew make the final preparations. Fifteen minutes later, I'm still running. I've definitely worked up more than a little sweat, and I'm on my own in the Namib desert. Briefly, I contemplate doing a Forrest Gump—keeping on right across the continent to Mozambique—but the crew catch up with me before the practicalities of not carrying my passport do.

Closeup shots of me lip synching are needed, and I must drive the Land Rover while Stuart hangs from the side of the van, running alongside with the camera. This means I have to use the old dirt road that is corrugated, full of rocks, and punctuated with vehicle-deep flash flood channels gouged from it as it runs parallel with the new tarmac highway at a steady and exact sixty kph while lip synching. I'm not sure whether the rest of the band trust me implicitly or have no idea that I feel like our last moments on Earth will be spent miming as we plough steadily and exactly into a gully, a ludicrous fate finely documented on film. The stock depletes before we bungle off this mortal coil.

On the night to celebrate the end of filming, we drive to Walvis Bay and a place called The Raft, a bar and restaurant built on a jetty in the town's lagoon. The nearby docks employ the local population, many of whom cannot swim, and a corpse floating serenely underneath but still in clear view of the revellers somewhat tarnished The Raft's opening night. With the quantity of alcohol consumed tonight, it's just a matter of time before one of us ends up drunk in the drink. I eat a jalapeno shark fillet, on the basis I should eat dangerous animals before they eat me, an approach I've utilised the world over with a variety of toothy fish, crocodile, bear, alligator, and kangaroo (okay, not strictly a predator, but try and find an Australian animal that isn't lethally poisonous)—a very appetising method of self-preservation.

We couldn't film the final planned adrenaline-inducing activity and could therefore attempt it at full throttle; quad-biking. These four-wheel drive, 200cc motorbikes conjure up the delinquent teenager in anyone. Within our first moments of what was supposedly a guided tour, Iain pulled doughnuts in the gravel, Ben from the crew took a flying jump at speed and buried the bike in a minor dune, Stuart had come over all speedway, and Jerry, well, joyfully unravelled the mysteries of piloting a motorised vehicle for the first time.

The guided element of the tour comes into its own when you head from the start area by the road and move into the desert. The gravel flats are sensitive ecological areas, tyre marks can be visible for decades afterwards (unlike in the dunes where the next day, our tracks were all but gone) and so the group sticks to existing trails, not that this is restrictive. In a speed tuck, in sixth gear and at the maximum speed of ninety kph, racing the rest of the group in a storm of dust, you don't feel particularly nannied. Then it's into the dunes where the manoeuvrability and power of the bikes makes them perfect for the terrain. The speed and G-forces involved in firing up an eighty-metre dune on the left side, riding along the crescent edge of the summit and then plummeting down the right-hand side to the valley leading to the next dune, are exhilarating. Through the sand mountains, tilting at crazy angles to the left then the right, dropping down forty-five-degree slopes, getting air, wheel spinning through slaloms, climbing impossible-looking faces of sand equals two hours of sand-spewing, grit-in-the-eyes, throttle-bashing heaven.

A couple of hours of this wasn't enough for me. I returned on our last day, a few hours before the return drive to Windhoek and the flight home, and tagged along with a group of Americans—school friends on an extended trip around southern Africa. After the briefing, a period of getting to know the controls on the bike is recommended, easing your way into the forthcoming ride. Within the first sixty seconds of this warm up, one of the women in the group had hit a couple of ridges at unfamiliar speed, tipped the bike back-over-front, faceplanted, and had the bike come down on her, breaking her collarbone. The ambulance took half an hour to arrive.

Twenty minutes later, having travelled a few short miles at speeds golf cart drivers would sneer at, one of the bikes breaks down with a clutch problem. During the forty minutes it takes for them to dispatch a replacement, one of the riders says of his friend, "I hate to say I told you so, but he said you don't need to use the clutch on these things." This, I feel, the bike manufacturers would not fully agree with. Two hours and many, many gear changes later, the same rider asked me how to select Neutral. The fact that he purposely chose a manual gearbox when automatics were readily available only heightens the mystery.

At about this point, the "What do you do?" questions start, and their knowledge of an old hit song of mine brings out the cameras again. "Hey! Can you sing the words to the song while I take the picture?" says one of my fellow bikers. Things become tense for a while.

After a great delay, my mind on the four-hundred-kilometre drive I should have already started, we were about to reach the halfway point. The guide, with me on his tail, descends the first of the dunes, hits a jump, and coasts to a halt on a gravel flat. We turn around to watch the arrival of the first rider behind us—the diplomatic photographer, who hits the jump, lands, turns around to look at it, and tips the bike onto its side, speedily introducing his face to the grittier side of Namibia. Very, very quietly, I decipher the guide saying, "Not again!" He has never had a "faller" before. Faller #2 this morning, but for the presence of ears, looks like he has done five rounds with Mike Tyson—his left eye swollen and bloody and cuts leaking all over his visage.

As they patch him, the rest of the crew are pootling towards the dune. The last of them, the second woman, attempts the seventy-metre-high, steep-sided lump of sand in a too-high gear with low revs and even less speed, if such tender velocity can be referred to as such. It's an interesting yet utterly useless approach. She stalls, axle deep, about a third of the way up. With the guide busy staunching Gravel Face's wounds and my flight imminent, I scoot to the bottom of the dune where I accelerate away again without getting trapped in the sand myself, climbing the slope, and haul the immobilised bike from the sand.

Another bike is heading our way, across the gravel, then up the dune.

Keep going! KEEP GOING! I'm screaming to myself, but telepathy fails me, and the second bike pulls to a stop almost on top of us, oblivious to the slope, the sand, and the limitations of both bike and rider.

"Hey! What's up?"

Well, what's up is I'm digging you lot from this bloody great dune one at a time while a couple of Air Namibia pilots tap their fingers on the black box, and the air hostesses grow steely eyed and spiteful, vengefully awaiting my eventual arrival. Freed, the woman attempts the same dune in the same manner with the same result.

The pattern for the remainder of this epic ride is set. Half of us will hammer up the dunes like the Banana Splits with road rage, reach the top, pause expectantly while looking over our shoulders, then switch the engines off, watch the guide disappear behind us, to emerge five minutes later, towing a Sunday driver of the future.

And so, my exit from Namibia is an overamped rush of part exhilaration, part panic. The accelerator pedal in the van remains stuck frantically to the floor as desert turns slowly into scrub, then bushveld, and our snail-like progress is made across the vast landscape. We tear past giraffe, springbok, and jackal. Our attention is occasionally drawn to traffic police and vice versa. The final surge comes from one last explosive, Technicolor sunset over Windhoek. Then the night fades out Namibia for me. The journey ends, and I'm drained of energy, ready for sleep.

Fat chance.

The Relative forces of Evil

My brother and his family paid a visit to London not long after I had returned. This was terrible news. It's not that I dislike my brother, it's just he's the Harbinger of Doom for my career. He left Britain just before things really took off for the band, working as a teacher in Zimbabwe (coincidentally, a neighbour state to Namibia), and there he met his future wife. Having erratically followed my career on the BBC World Service, they returned suspiciously in time to witness things start to go wrong in the *Perverse* era. Having moved to Barbados, they were on holiday in greater numbers—two children strengthening the Forces of Darkness—just as things got really bad for us.

I went round to see them on a rare (and deceptively?) sunny evening, taking the new video with me so they could get wistfully nostalgic at the southern African scenery and to show the kids that Uncle Mike went to the desert to sit in a deck chair and sing. Only once did a malign undercurrent show itself when my three-year-old nephew got rowdy at not being allowed to go out and get the Indian take-away.

To be fair, I would have done the same in his place.

U's that? In this?

Speaking of the Dark Side, I'd been fraternising with the mountain bikers' enemy-within-cycling, the road cyclist, and bought a road bike. It was part of the range by ex-Tour de France champion, Greg LeMond—the Alpe d'Huez model, named after a bloody great hill in the south of France where he'd had to slog out his guts for a few Tours running. I would have been more likely to call the bike, Oh Jesus, Not That Monster Again!

In July 1997, the Tour de France transversed that climb, and one drunken night with some cycling friends, we decided to hire a car, borrow tents, drive hideous hours, watch the Tour go past, and I'd get to do a variation on taking coals to Newcastle and up the Alpe d'Huez, on an Alpe d'Huez.

And so we left London on an early Thursday evening and drove for six hundred and fifty miles through the night. By the time we got to Grenoble, it was 8 a.m. on Friday. I'd refused to relinquish the steering wheel even for a moment and was wild-eyed with Red Bull and coffee. Still, I managed a couple of hours sleep before the heat of the sun drove me from the oven-like tent. Ten minutes later, the rain drove me inside again, and nature's little practical joke continued this amusing cycle until we'd all had enough and decided, like true Brits abroad, to go to a bar in the nearby town.

Six months earlier, I'd have expected July to have been a time of touring and interviews, stuck in a tour bus en route to Leicester or Cleveland or Hamburg. Instead, I sunned myself in southern France, drinking wine and about to witness the biggest, most glamorous bike race in the world. Even in decline, (ex) rock stardom wasn't too shabby.

"Let's ride up the hill"

By midnight, we felt very relaxed and confident—cocky, even. And so, someone uttered the clarion call of the weekend, "I know! Let's ride up the hill." The "hill" is one of the the most notorious climbs on the Tour de France—fourteen kilometres long, featuring twenty-one hairpin bends and five thousand feet of altitude gain. It's one of the few climbs of the tour graded "beyond expectation," which shows how badly it translates from French, since after you've done it once, you have all too clear an expectation—expectation of pain and suffering (why else would all these spectators come?). It is the mountain the riders on the Tour fear most, the ascent all other road climbs are compared to. It's unlikely those supreme athletes would know this, but I can assure them and the world the first three wall-like hairpins are an extremely effective cure for drunkenness.

Two of us struggled up this piece of bravado road building, with drunken Danes, Germans, Italians, Dutch, Spanish, and French cheering us on. They were part of the five million spectators who came to watch the race, spewing (sometimes literally) from high-altitude beer tents and singing those hyper-jolly summer Euro hits—records with that soft-end-of-techno beat and words of no discernible language and no discernible consonants repeated until everyone falls down drunk, a cross between a football chant, a beer-drinking song, and the *Teletubbies*. I rode through this thinking, "I am Martin Sheen on a bike. This is the remake of *Apocalypse Now*." (Never get off the bike, absolutely goddamn right!)

Half frozen and exhausted, we careered down from the top at 2 a.m., sliding almost out of control on the freshly painted slogans the fans daubed on the road to spur their tortured heroes the next day.

"Let's ride up the hill"

Six hours later, we did it again in the heat of the morning and in the midst of a large army of spectators traveling by car, bike, and foot. Despite the blazing sun, it wasn't warm enough at the summit for anything more than a coffee and a baguette before zipping down the hill to wait for the arrival of the Tour at the bottom of the climb.

Perched on our rocky corner twenty feet above the road, we watched the ludicrous cavalcade of sponsors' and advertisers' vehicles cruise past. They had decorated the cars like the products (my favourite was the giant mobile cheese) with Barbie-doll women tossing free promotional tack and more of that lost-consonant Europop blaring out. It was two hours of Carnival meets Disney meets Coca-Cola.

As the race officials' cars, police, and support vehicles slowly replaced the procession of kitsch, we heard the helicopter that films the riders traversing the valley. It circled above the town of Le Bourg d'Oisans, and the clamour died away, and the sense of expectation was palpable.

The false starts of motorbike camera teams and police escorts built the tension. We saw them at the far end of the approach road. The shimmering movement of the riders and the bright colours of bikes and team jerseys made the peleton mirage-like as the teams jockeyed for position, keeping the pace as high as possible in order to hurl their chosen rider up the start of the hill and break the will of competitors preparing themselves for the ordeal. The speed the group maintained as it bore down on us was phenomenal. For a fleeting moment, the riders zipped in front of and below me and rounded the corner to start the climb—a mass of bodies moving and sweating, bikes clicking and whirring. It was an eerily quiet flash of muscle, sinew, flesh, titanium, aluminium, carbon fibre, and plastic—one that fires by like a single, giant organism.

At this point and at this speed, it was just about impossible to discern the individuals riders, but the look of concentration and anxiety was the same on all their faces. In a second, the group passed us, and the team support cars bunched behind. In the middle of the cars, a lone rider fought the traffic to rejoin the main group. He got the biggest cheer of the day.

We watched the rest of the race in a bar two hundred yards away. The Italian, Marco Pantani, won the stage, climbing the Alpe d'Huez in thirty-eight minutes—an average of 18mph.

Imagine the steepest hill you know extending for eight miles, and then imagine cycling that at an average of 18mph. Maybe just try doing 18mph on the flat first.

Fleas can jump distances in vast multiples of their body length and height due to a phenomenal strength-to-weight ratio. I suspect a radioactive flea had bitten Mr. Pantani in his youth, and instead of a life spent fighting crime (well, face it, as "Fleaman," criminals are unlikely to take you seriously), he thrashes up hills on bikes for a living.

I'd reached the summit in an hour. In my favour, Marco Pantani didn't have to contend with stationery buses and half a million foolhardy pedestrians in the road. In his favour, I hadn't had to cycle up a slow incline for one hundred miles before I'd even reached the mountain (does driving 650 miles count?) on an afternoon under a clear Mediterranean sky.

We'll call it a draw then.

"Let's ride up the hill"

Yes, again—the third time in twenty-four hours. We'd sat outside a restaurant and watched the traffic snaking down the hill for five hours after the race had finish, the lights marking their long, slow crawl as darkness descended.

The ascent was easier in the cool of night, but it's never easy. The gradient taunts you. Too steep to require anything other than maximum effort, too long to provide any easing of the pace, it's all or nothing. We had no lights other than the stars. A traffic cop on the almost-deserted road stopped us, but the sound of our crap French invoked a tone of weary resignation, and he looked away, fed up. Sometimes it's good to be British.

The descent was one of the best rides of my life. The full moon illuminated the road so well I'd probably have been worse off with bike lights. I could see the grey of the road in front, the trees on either side, and the end of each hairpin. With no people about, very little traffic, and all the paint dried from the day's sun, nothing could stop me.

At some point, I hit 40mph, probably overtaking a car on one of the longer straights. By the last few hairpins, the vehicles behind me perfectly illuminated the road, and the warm air from the valley rejuvenated the feeling to my fingers and toes— a celebratory warmth to match the rush of the descent.

We drove for fourteen hours the next day, going home with the undersides of the bikes covered in a bizarre pattern of different-coloured paint from the road. A fine memento.

Oh yes, one other thing. The second single was imminent, the album's release got closer, and I had so little to do that I might just as well have followed the rest of the Tour.

At the end of July, I did a Japanese phoner and a short regional press interview. That was the sum of the month's promotion.

11.

August

Bang!

August started with a bang—two interviews in a single day! One of them was for Teletext, so that was our TV campaign fully covered. No photographer attended, but then I remembered they'd probably draw a pixel diagram of my face instead.

Whimper

I had started a diary to aid my memory, since someone had suggested I write a book about the year we were having. It was a crazy idea, but I thought that it might just work. My entry for Monday the fourth states simply, *"Chemical #1" released—I'd almost forgotten, and I'm sure the world doesn't know. Even Teletext slagged it.*

The bastards! And I bet my face in pixels had the wrong eye colour too. Being slagged on Teletext is a bit like being beaten up by a granny. It's the sort of thing that shouldn't happen to anyone, least of all grown men. Imagine *Hello* magazine describing one of their subjects as "a rich, tasteless, upper-class twat with an obvious genetic disorder." I was that surprised with a Teletext-ual drubbing.

Nothing to See Here

In effect, all we did was wait—waited to see how the American deal turned out, waited to see if we were headed to Japan, waited for the predictable farce of the album's release to play out at home, waited to see what would happen then.

The rest of the band had spent the last four years becoming consummate killers of time, and now I had big gaps in my diary for the first time in a decade. It was a strange and uneasy feeling for me. I liked to keep every minute of every day full, sometimes subconsciously defeating an occasional will to relax. I followed a couple of leads and started serious work on some website designs so once again I could spend long hours in front of a computer, feeling occupied.

My social life improved, and I spent most nights of the first week of August either going out or meeting friends at home—friends who worked in journalism or press representation. I wasn't the only one surprised at our lack of press.

Apolog

The Big Phone Call

At the height of our success, the phone had hardly stopped ringing. Gail would call at least once a day, Food less often but still frequently. They were numbers 1 and 2 on the speed dial function of my phone.

On the day of "Chemical #1"'s second disastrous midweek—the record industry has decreed Thursday is also the middle of the week—I got my first call of the month from Gail (I hadn't heard from Food since June). EMI's head of A&R had called to ask her if it was worth releasing a third single or "are Jesus Jones played out?" It seemed if an intimation existed, EMI would still be interested in keeping me.

Me, not the band.

Gail had left them with the consideration that it was only worthwhile releasing another single if they could guarantee serious play on the radio. The song being mooted as the potential single was the first track I'd written for the album and one of the songs that had prompted the "great, but where are the singles" comment three years before.

Sometime in the summer, we'd been offered a Russian gig on part of the bill at a large festival in a stadium east of Moscow. In our experience and from what we'd heard about eastern Europe, it was likely to be a riot of chaos and disorganisation, but hey! It was a free trip to Russia, another stamp in the by-now-technicoloured pages of the passport, another country crossed off the list of places yet to be played. We had agreed to do it despite the lack of details or contract, and I'd even done an interview for Russian TV about it.

The interview proved every bit as ramshackle as I'd expected. It took place at Abbey Road Studios, where the studio management gave the grand tour to the headliners—a Russian ensemble well into their forties—for the benefit of the accompanying camera crew. As I arrived, they emerged onto the steps outside, and a raging argument that sounded like it was of the "But I was supposed to sit where Ringo sat!" variety heated the studio foyer. The English-speaking voices were obviously the translator and the guys with the sound and camera equipment. From the rest of the dozen or so people, I found it difficult to guess who the official interviewer was. Until a pretty woman with a microphone momentarily emerged from the melee.

For two minutes, a crowd that in news reporting would qualify as an angry mob shouted at me in Russian. Those who stuck the backs of their heads in front of each other and the camera, I took to be asking questions. Those who retorted angrily, I took to be answering for me. Once in a while the translator would ask me something in English over the clamour, and I looked in vain for the woman with the microphone while quoting from the Prince Charles book of *Speak While Baffled by Noisy Foreigners* along the lines of "Very much looking forward to …," "Great opportunity …," and "Who the bloody hell is asking me this …?"

Suddenly, four blokes looking like my uncle stood in a line and put their arms around me while the camera filmed us. That sorted out who the band was. Then the shouting started again as they all walked back and forth across that zebra crossing, and I was off on my bike.

August was when the festival organisers realised the event required capital and cancelled it with less than a month to go.

Patient Still Alive, Prepare Funeral

My sinister road-cycling fetish increased, and I spent Thursday evenings averaging 26mph and six inches behind the wheel of another cyclist on a custom-built circuit in West London. Returning shattered from one of these sessions, Dave Balfe pulled me over in his flashy company car.

While Andy Ross was who'd taken us to Food, Dave was who'd been leaving the office when he heard the demo of "Info Freako" and had said, "Sign them!" once the first chorus accompanied him putting on his coat. The few things Dave and I didn't see eye to eye on, we'd enjoy arguing about. Interestingly for me, Dave's disenchantment with both music and the industry had happened at the same time as mine, but where I'd ground on like a gloomy production line, Dave had left Food to sum up, enjoy the countryside, and play Doom for eight hours a day. Now, though, he was back in the fray, heading a department at one of the major labels.

He commiserated with "Chemical #1"'s feeble midweek and had plenty of advice on my solo career—one I hadn't even considered by then. His final advice of "Never doubt your talent" may sound glib out of context, but at that point, it was an eye-opener that bordered on a revelation for me. It took something like that—the right words from the right person at the right time—to realise the last six years of doing nothing but doubting my own talent had beaten the crap from me. Now, with the imminent death of the album, I freed myself from that.

The next morning, Gail called to say the head of A&R and the CEO of EMI UK wanted to take the two of us to dinner. This would almost certainly be about a solo career since you don't get taken out to dine with the big wigs in South Kensington to be told you're no longer on the label—think of the doggy bag you'd take home if you did. Our contract expired in October, and the intimation was I'd sign a new deal. Although they mentioned nothing definite and did not discuss terms. On one hand, the chance that, for me, the uncertainty would end and the good life would continue was a relief. On the other, knowing the album had been written off before release (the funeral arrangements prepared before the death of the patient) and what that would mean for the rest of the band negated any euphoria at the thought of being offered a new deal.

That night I went out with a group of friends, including Andy Ross. It started as an amiable evening and ended as an ugly, drunken mess, having to leave a Soho club early before a friend got us all thrown out for crawling over the other clubbers' tables to sit on the edge of a four-storey-high wall.

Chemical #1

"Chemical #1" was not a success in its first and final week. Thank God we got a fun video shoot from it. The same conversation that delivered the single's results also featured Gail's opinion that we wouldn't be going to Japan.

Gen had visited Japan for his daughter's birth and had been with our Toshiba EMI rep. It seemed the company there weren't giving the album much attention. Some interdepartmental politicking had occurred, which didn't help the fact they weren't happy with the delay of the album. That the Anglophile section of Japanese rock fans had read virtually nothing about us from the usual sources meant even less enthusiasm from Toshiba.

We learned via the back door that the album wasn't a priority. As a result, they offered us one gig in Tokyo. It wouldn't even be enough money to cover the cost of flying there, let alone hotels, wages, and rehearsals.

With the single's plight at home and the US collapse, I'd thought a tour of Japan was the one dependable thing. After all, I'd been there for every year of the decade but one, mostly touring but with a couple of DJ stints in '95 and '96. The home situation had been foreseeable, the American one unbelievable and not yet over, but for Japan to fall through with such little drama was a crushing blow, and still for me, one of the two saddest points in a year of disappointments.

Maybe it's the similarity in the national characteristics of the two island nations of England and Japan: the repression, the diffidence, the extreme venting of that. Perhaps it's the simultaneously reassuring and thrillingly strange nature of a western culture laid transparently over the top of a radically different one. Maybe it's a gadget fiend's love of technology.

Maybe it's an admiration for the single-minded determination, with which so many of my Japanese friends follow their interests. Maybe it's just the shallowness of being treated like a bona-fide rock star, even if you're there to play to just one hundred and fifty people. Whatever it was, I'm still deeply saddened at not playing *Already* in Japan.

Not at One with Modern Technology

The World Wide Web took over my life. I spent most of my days in August working on websites, eagerly experimenting with graphics software in the same way I'd toyed with digital music hardware, getting the technology to do the donkey work and being free to discover new imagery or sounds. In the past, I'd made songs that didn't feature any musical interments, relying on the natural pitch of whatever I'd sampled to provide the key. Now I designed unique virtual shapes and objects or created bits of metal, paper, or plastic on the computer screen that didn't exist in the real world. Fun with machinery, once more.

The Jesus Jones website received a request for an interview with me from an online music and culture magazine. They'd come to the website after approaching EMI and being told they couldn't have an interview because EMI had yet to develop a policy on internet fanzines. In April, I'd done a trio of fanzine interviews with readership figures possibly in the hundreds. It was estimated that four million people in the UK had internet access during this time period, and I had seen estimates of the world-wide figure—and the internet is, after all, global—at around one hundred sixty million in 1997.

I did the interview.

Rta Catcher

Other emails arrived via the website, along with letters from the fan club. Mostly, these were from people who'd begin the message by being embarrassed at writing to a favourite musician and apologising for praising me, as though compliments would somehow irritate me and demean the sender. This displays an acute misunderstanding of the kind of people who want to become famous in the first place, I feel.

Not all the letters were even-tempered though. The stranger letters could be funny—like the outlines of a fan's penis drawn in various stages of erection—or they could be a little too dark for comfort.

I'd been sent a few long, rambling letters from a fan who felt his relationship with me was far greater than I could see justification for. *Perverse* was a direct message to him, for example, as explained by the numerology involved in the lyrics. He sent a mocking letter in reply to me when (reading from another of Prince Charles's books) I explained I didn't quite see what he meant, but since he'd bought the album, he could read into it whatever he liked. The next I'd heard from him was through a series of desperate telegrams sent into the fan club that unfortunately took advantage of a slow year by rarely collecting the mail. I got the messages saying he had to resolve the situation, or he didn't know what would happen. He insisted I meet him, after he had flown halfway around the world to London and long after I'd heard from Gail that he'd waited outside her office for many hours, asking for my address.

In August, more messages arrived. He was coming to London again, penniless, and I had to meet him. This is supposed to happen to the likes of John Lennon or Steven Spielberg or Whitney Houston, and here I was with two failed singles and a buried-alive album—very far from being a megastar in the public eye.

Something was wrong with this picture.

Chinatown

Something was also wrong with my love life, but that would be expected with a girlfriend living in New York. Still on first name terms with the immigration staff at Heathrow, she'd flown to see me in February, April, and June, usually for a long weekend each time, which she considered less than perfect. I had to agree. To try and even the air miles, I'd decided to go there regularly.

I escaped an education in the numerology of my lyrics by fleeing to New York four days before *Already*'s release. This seems incredible to me now—not that I finally got chivalrous but that the band's spokesman was free to disappear during the week of the album's release. But then, absolutely nothing was promoting it, and its failure was a foregone conclusion that didn't merit any attention.

In the sweltering heat of Manhattan in August, amidst the stink of Chinatown's open fish markets and through the smoke of the pool halls my girlfriend cherished as I did bike races, I contemplated the band's last chance—America—as the album began its steep nosedive in the shops at home. The money we'd made in record sales had always gone towards our wages and tours, keeping us from debt with the record company, but in the four years since we'd sold any records, we'd steadily ploughed through that cash. The wages probably wouldn't last the rest of year. The latest estimate for the American schedule would be a February release with a tour in March, and if the rest of the band had to get jobs, how would we tour? It was hard escaping depressing thoughts that summer, wherever I flew to.

In London, Jerry was partly jubilant at getting a one-year suspended sentence for his drug charge and partly philosophical at the album's unconvincing encounter with the Top 200. The rest of the band now knew EMI might be thinking of re-signing me without them. His view was that I should do it since it was better that one of us got something from it than none. And, as Gail put it, other record companies were hardly beating down the door to sign us.

Nothing fails like failure.

Bomb

The album bombed completely, so much so that British fans still contacted the fan club throughout 1998, asking when *Already* would be released. At the time, it had ceased to be important and didn't figure in my day-to-day life, because I blocked out thoughts of it. It was humiliating to go out that way, and my response was to ignore the situation.

As the year progressed, the sadness of the defeat crept up on me, along with the futility of all that effort: the agony and joy and soul searching of writing, the months and months of recording, Martyn's attention to detail, and the optimism in the studio. Then I regretted doing so much stuff that seemed like hard work: the inane questions from bored interviewers in tiny radio stations and the interviews on autopilot. I might just as well have gone biking for half the year, stayed in Namibia, got around to all those unread books from many Christmases past, taken my daughter on a road trip of the USA, lived with my girlfriend in New York, or taken up full-contact origami. But then, the trouble with having a work ethic like the bright-red writing through a stick of rock was it would happen.

There was confusion too. In the week of its abysmal first and last chart position, *Already* got a great review in the *Times*. Was its fate deserved or outrageous? I see flaws in the album: too many mid-paced songs, not enough oomph, too dark, some dodgy lyrics. But then, how many Top 20 albums don't suffer from most, if not all, of those flaws? No, I'd done it all to the full. I'd rewritten when it was necessary, forcing myself to do the best I could at the time. I'd not been lazy and sloppy in the studio. I'd done all the promotion asked of me and been ready and prepared for much more.

I still listen to that album and enjoy it. *Already* is a good album.

12.

SEPTEMBER
Musique Non Stop

I worked on web stuff full time, enjoying the days being creative without the concerns of rhyming or over-familiar chord changes. Hours manipulating imagery meant that, for the first time in years, I had long stretches of time to listen to music in a situation where I could concentrate on it, have a part of my mind open to consider, to analyse and revel in it.

As ever, I taped radio shows—two-hour DATs of the *Kiss Jungle Show*, the *Evening Session*, and John Peel from Radio 1, XFM, and speed garage—a genre of electronica dance music associated with the UK garage scene—from pirate radio. Albums by DJ Krust, the Bloodhound Gang, Ed Rush, Soul Coughing, Natasha Atlas, Spearhead, Roni Size, Squarepusher, Aphex Twin, Dead Can Dance, Lamb, a speed garage compilation CD, and *The Songs of Popular Islam* filled the gaps between radio tapes and often had me leaping from the computer to grab a guitar, figure out an inspiring chord change, and jam a few variations.

Ten minutes later, I'd have forgotten the improvised bit, but it still felt good for new music to excite me again.

"If you ever need a guitarist ..."

I hadn't told the rest of the band about EMI's overtures since there wasn't much to tell at this point. What little we knew I didn't feel had to be kept secret, and Gail had given them what information we had whenever they were in contact.

Jerry's attitude was "Good luck to you. And if you ever need a guitar player ..." Iain was less ambiguous, ringing me every couple of days to find out the latest and unimpressed with EMI's approach, which I find easy to understand. Al lived in Chicago, and I didn't hear from him much. His inability with the fax machine and my inability with late-night phone calls (swerving around the time difference) limited contact.

The only answer I had for all of them was that until we'd had a release in what had been our biggest market in the world, Jesus Jones took precedence over anything else for me. As the one who put the most effort, the most of myself into the album, I'd be the one to hammer the last nail in the coffin before walking away from it.

End of Season Transfers

The restaurant where Gail and I met Neil and JF from EMI had been, up until a little over a week before, one of Lady Diana's regular haunts. It wasn't an East End Balti House, in case you wondered. I was allowed to order from the wine list, and despite the faux pas of ordering a New World red in the presence of a Frenchman, it was a success. It was unlikely the barkeep stocked the cellars with truly dreadful vintages however, so I didn't swell too much at my social prowess.

A popular caricature of record company people portrays them as greed-crazed, oleaginous fiends set on the destruction of all that is good in music via their apocalyptically bland, big-selling automaton artists, with coke habits like Pacino's in *Scarface* fuelling their evil machinations. When I turn this into a screenplay, that will be the case. In the non-dramatised world, you need a politically Machiavellian nature to head a large music corporation, but to gain a reputation as "an artist's man," as JF has, you need an entirely different sensibility also. Neil had worked with us for years as our record plugger until his move to EMI a few weeks before, and so instead of table slamming, ultimatums, threats, cajolery, Faustian scheming, and dialogue straight from *The Bodyguard*, the four of us ate and drank and talked about music, France, Diana— dramatically deceased—and, oddly enough, bikes. It took Gail to get steely eyed and say, "So why are we here?"

It was a matter of transferring, not dropping, apparently. For me, I'd be transferred from one deal to another—no need to discuss the details now. With the new deal, I could do what I wanted, whenever I wanted to do it—no sooner than six months, no later than three years. This did look more promising than cycle couriering. For the rest of the band, it wasn't so jolly, and despite the happy talk, I felt deeply uneasy. The transfer for them was from on the label to off the label. Part of the deal was that I could work with whomever I liked, but the press and radio stand-off made it seem like all the members of Jesus Jones under another name stood about the same chance as Salman Rushdie disguised as an Ayatollah on a literary tour of Iran. "*Plus ça change,*" Iain, our Latin degree'd linguistics expert, might well have thought, since I was the band's writer and spokesman. However, the gamble that the press might go for the angle of me solo seemed surer than risking any more on the band, no doubt. As a bonus, I could stay with Food—now wholly owned by EMI—if I wanted, and for reasons of sentiment, loyalty, and belief in Andy Ross's manifesto for the label, I did want to stay.

When Iain called before ten o'clock the next day and Jerry shortly after, I had to explain the brutal reality that I had a deal which excluded them. I didn't mention the transfer euphemism—it was bad enough without that. The only way I felt better about it was by repeating that I'd give the album my all in America. If it took off there, then EMI would have to reconsider their position here. Splitting us up was out of the question just because we no longer had a deal in the UK, but it was still a heart-wrenching position to be in. If I stood steadfastly behind the band, told EMI it was all of us or nothing, well, nothing it would be for all of us. We had no other interest at all, and it was Gail's opinion that even on my own, other record companies would demand demos from me before considering an offer. I'd be where I had been a decade earlier.

The future of the band became both clearer and bleaker. A small amount of money remained in the band account, and with no foreseeable income, it was time to wind up the business partnership. Within a month, we'd be out of contract and no longer a trading company.

My amorous partnership also waned. In London, my head was full of things to occupy it every minute of the day, from the band's plight, to getting website contracts, to being a single parent. In New York, my girlfriend worked a job she hated and faced the hopelessness of a relationship that in the long term looked to only benefit American Airlines. Nothing definite was said, but I sensed a gradual distancing, like ship from shore, and felt that familiar sick, adolescent panic. September would be the month to consider decline and finality as the temperature fell and the days shrank with the year's ageing.

The year, the band, and even the racing—the last big event of the summer featured a crash near the start where two riders required medical assistance—all looked equally as bleak. A hilariously weak quote from my diary says, *Some year this is turning out to be.* I hope I wrote that one in my sleep.

In the last of the morbidity, Dave Balfe rang Gail to say he'd heard we were splitting up and wanted to invite himself to the party. Maybe sometime in the indeterminate future Dave can have invite #1.

food forrogo

At the end of the month, Food held a party to coincide with their "100 Singles Released" celebratory CD, and the band, having made a sizeable chunk of that 100, were invited. Iain had a DJ gig the same night at the Good Mixer in Camden, a pub well known as the Blur/Food hangout shortly before their rise to massive popularity. It was just along the road from the party venue, so I'd arranged to stop by on my way.

Inside, Food had posters covering the pub walls, celebrating the label and the CD. Waiting for my change at the bar, I scanned the posters and checked off the bands. "Blur, yep, Shampoo, Dubstar, Octopus, Grass Show, The Supernaturals, a very hard-to-make-out photo of ... Strangelove. And ... that's it." Where the hell were we?

It's an ugly thing to do, to persecute someone in the middle of their celebrations, and I didn't feel happy about being the party pooper, but I felt even less happy about the insult of the poster.

"It's not my fault," Andy protested.

"So, whose is it?"

"Um, well, uh, I suppose it is me who should take ultimate responsibility. I don't really have an explanation."

I didn't care whose fault it was. I didn't care what was said much either. The album had been out for just five weeks; we were still on the label; we were on the CD; and I was supposed to sign a new deal with Food soon. What could they lose by including us? Did we have to be so publicly disowned?

Ten minutes later, Jo from Food approached and asked—since Andy and many of the bands on the label were in the immediate area—if I'd join in with the photos. In the light of the situation, I found that a little difficult to swallow. The rant that followed touched on the notion that if we were not good enough in public, the private photos could go to hell. This, after all, was the label I'd enthused about in so many interviews, explaining it wasn't like any other label in the friendliness and approachability. If we'd been signed direct to, say, Polygram in 1988, this would have been a likely eventuality, but we signed to Food because we thought they wouldn't be just another cynical corporation. And now, when it came to the crunch, it was the big corporation that stood by me while Food couldn't wait to deny their involvement. It would have been more decent to "disappear" us altogether—remove us from the CD too and take away some of those tracks that had financed the new offices, more staff, the new lifestyle, made the EMI buyout an attractive proposition—and erase from history the sleeve note quotes that went along the lines of "it was Jesus Jones that put Food on the map."

For many weeks afterwards, the snubbing greatly depressed me. It still saddens me now (although I'm unable to hold a grudge), and even greater than not visiting Japan for one last tour, it was the single worst event of that miserable year. If the album bombs, forces outside your control are involved. When a friend stiffs you, it just doesn't compare. Not quite the words of Jesus, but rumour has it he wasn't that impressed with Judas, if I can throw in some historical weighting.

Other than a mute and drunken nuzzling soon after my rant about the photo, Andy made no contact afterwards, despite his (reportedly) anxious request to JF that I stay on Food. I compared the phone calls and meetings with Dave Balfe and JF throughout the summer with Food's silence. I discussed with Gail the lack of interest and the rebuff of the poster. Didn't it seem stupid to remain on Food?

She called Andy to let him know that my party pooping was more than a tantrum and could be a bigger event than he appeared to realise. His response, apparently, was "Yes, Gail," in the manner you use on your mother when she tells you, thirty years on, to wrap up warm and eat well.

13.

OCTOBER

Sawtooth Mike I.

I flew out of Gatwick, bound once more for New York, and into a deceptively innocuous, cloudless sky. The placid weather did nothing to calm my habitual take-off terror, which had me inadvertently ripping the armrests away from the seat and leaning with pathetic futility to counteract the suicidal turns the pilot seemed to put the aircraft through. Just my luck to get the itchy ex-test pilot. Again. Hadn't he heard of wind shear and been aware of our chances of slipping sideways out of the sky to be at one with the soil of Surrey? It would at least strike an emotive note in the bike press if I descended onto one of my regular race courses below, and I found myself considering whether my body, strapped religiously into the seat at all times, would present an interesting technical challenge to the racers of the future.

For a decade, I'd lived with a diary that overflowed like a well-shaken champagne bottle when it seemed like I really only had time to tend to life's essentials—the things seemingly necessary to keep my world turning for another twenty-four hours, including mountain biking. Going to the dentist, that popular pastime for us all, was not high on the list and often inconvenient four weeks into an American tour. But wouldn't you know it, my mother's advice returned to haunt me. In the last couple years, I'd noticed my teeth becoming sensitive, then painful, and later, occasionally bloody. However, I was made of stern stuff and stoically ignored the dental-danger signs. Inevitably, the decline came, and in the summer, one of my eye teeth raced ahead of the others in its decay, suffering visibly. At the start of summer's collapse into autumn, a small part of it came away, and although painless, the sharp edge of the break was a constant source of cuts to my tongue, which found the exploration of this exciting new dental feature irresistible. I'd realised as I biked through London—usually somewhere very public, like Oxford Street—that I'd be pulling grotesque facial contortions as the ceaselessly fascinating tooth snared my tongue over and over.

On this nervy flight to New York, I performed a routine inspection of the razor-edged beast when I discovered, like an eager archaeologist unearthing a skull in the Rift Valley, a slight crack. Under attention, this widened and kept doing so until I realised, with a sense of bodily horror well known to Jeff Goldblum in *The Fly*, a larger piece of the tooth was coming away. That all of this was painless only heightened the sense of horrified unreality—maybe I could pitch this to David Cronenberg.

A recurring dream during the last few years had featured my teeth crumbling in my mouth, painlessly but messily, as though my mouth were full of tiny pieces of smooth gravel that I would spit out. I'd heard this was a typical singer's dream, but this was from another singer, a profession that often believes the more interesting human phenomena are its exclusive property. Whether it signifies anything—other than take your mum's advice and go to the dentist regularly—I don't know.

The film on the plane was *Austin Powers: International Man of Mystery*—a British character parodied, in part, for his terrible dentistry.

Escape to New York

It was a good time to get away from home. The web-design work had suffered a big setback when, after weeks' worth of effort on one major site, we discovered a separate part of the company had commissioned other designers, unaware of our efforts. I hope they paid a lot more than we were asking. I could work on other things, but by and large, I felt I worked not for results but just to be busy.

In previous years, I would have risked my flesh and the odd collar bone once more on a dusty bike trail somewhere, but despite the invitation to tour the Rocky Mountain states of America with friends and bikes, it felt like time to be less frivolous, time to start a new chapter in my life in a determined manner.

The Food farrago, my girlfriend's diplomatic embargo, the album's failure, the quandary with the band, the website disappointment—all this played on my mind and didn't make the darkening days any jauntier. It felt similar to when I'd been writing *Already*, waking up feeling fine but soon after breakfast a cloak of gloom and apathy would fall on me as I hammered away at the computer.

What an idiot! I should have gone to Utah, never mind the personal injury potential. Instead, I found New York wasn't much cooler in August and the smell of Chinatown fiercely undiminished. After a week of coffee, drinking, cinema, and still working on a computer, I came home to find winter's preparations well underway.

History Rewritten?

Gail, our illustrious manager, had her illustriousness recognised and furthered during the International Managers Forum Peter Grant Award held at the Hilton on Park Lane, Mayfair. Despite the title, this wouldn't be the sort of event where people got to throw TV sets from the window or make physical threats against business adversaries. Although that might have changed if Gail had learned sooner that she had won the award—she'd refused to accept it point blank for a couple of years running. This year she would be ambushed with it, and her coterie of bands were amongst the surprise guests to add to her embarrassment and make the acceptance speech a little fierier.

The Pretenders would be playing there anyhow (at the event, they're not the house band at the Hilton, don't go booking a room there just yet) so them being in the building wouldn't spoil the surprise. The rest of us had to sneak in and hide inside the hotel until the big moment, attempting to look just furtive enough to escape attention but not enough to be ejected from such a grand venue. By either a stroke of luck or with unerring ability, I found The Pretenders' dressing room just as the waitstaff began serving dinner—steak tartare, ho-ho. I followed the band to the backstage area. A large screen displaying each winner's accomplishments hid the dining-room guests as the super-confident voiceover boomed out the list of credits.

When Gail's turn came, I sat by a pile of guitar cases next to the guitar tuner, watching the screen from behind. The

Oscars-style introduction began: an overview of Gail's band-by-band from the early days of Charisma Records and Peter Hammill, taking in such luminaries as Peter Gabriel and Chrissie Hynde, and incorporating the latest Gailforce protégé, Bernard Butler. Food's month-old snub still flagellated my ego, and as one of the PAs rang out the names, I had a sickening feeling that, somehow, we'd be excluded from this too. Suddenly, it seemed like we were the lepers of the industry, the untouchables, the homeless on the streets of the big city—a failure's example to look the other way, look over, or look through, to keep a distance or be similarly cursed. And that goes to show how paranoid I'd got since we made it onto the randomly selected list, second from last in a long roll call. Still, it made me sweat.

The relief of still being publicly connected with at least some of the people we'd had success with probably prompted an even more enthusiastic assault on the free drinks than usual. The rest of the evening was a blur of chat with other bands, industry people, and old friends, as if nothing had changed in the last five years. It ended for me when the last few survivors of the evening suggested a trip to one of the West End's celebrated media haunts. I'd had a good run and didn't want to spoil it.

A Canterbury Tale

A far soberer evening came near the end of the month. I realised that by DJing I could recoup my money on all the techno 12"s

I had been buying in '92 and '93. At that time, the band's fame was enough to get club promoters to listen to me, and having proved myself, by '95, I played often, usually in London but also across England and in Japan (twice in two years). Iain, who'd DJed at university, joined me sometimes, and a friend, Joel, played all but the Japanese dates—fair reward for getting the gigs.

My enthusiasm for techno had been waning since about '94 when it no longer appeared to be the innovative force it had been, and drum 'n' bass rose from the ruins to steal the thunder. However, once we were known for playing one sound, we were booked to play it, whatever our tastes. Okay, so we could have found different clubs to play in, but that would have meant another club mafia to try and infiltrate for months or years on end, and I had other things to expend the energy on.

The result, after a few triumphant nights at the likes of Club UK or Sex, Love, and Motion at Soundshaft, was usually the sort of night we had in Canterbury: hiring a car to sit in traffic for an hour or so, belting down a motorway, listening to a tape and trying to remember which sounds connected with which labels, then ending up in a small club with a tiny number of half-interested people.

We'd try a little drum 'n' bass, which, in the words of a documentary, still seemed very much to be "A London T"ing," and then relent and play what people wanted to dance to later. "The bloody public!" as a manager and record label boss friend of mine likes to say. The pay at the end of the evening would never match the expenses, but there would always be a few moments of real joy in every evening—the music fan's dream of playing a favourite tune at phenomenal volume through a large PA without the neighbours complaining.

All in all, though, playing these nights under the banner of The Jesus Jones Sound System added to the sense of finality for the band.

Big Little Moment

Sometime in October, I don't care to know when, Food/EMI's option to renew the contract with Jesus Jones came up, and they let it pass. Silently, then, the deal that I'd focused so much of my life on, fixated upon while in teenage bands, daydreamed about during work in my twenties, the one that had given EMI one of their bigger successes of the early '90s, slipped into oblivion.

14.

NOVEMBER

Normal

Being free from a recording contract for the first time in nine years, my life was a very ordinary one, or so it seemed to me (especially if I disregarded flying to New York once a month). I was at a computer, if not nine to five, then hours that amounted to that, and racing or just riding bikes on the weekends. I was also occupied as a single parent for a week at a time each month, as I had been soon after my daughter's first birthday.

For the first year, I found parenthood unbelievably hard, trying to write whilst seldom sleeping more than a few hours and being both provider and entertainer for Hana. She didn't cheer like adult audiences did. As she grew older, she could speak and communicate, which solved so many simple problems, and I came to rely more on the au pairs imported to keep her Swedish heritage in working condition. Her ability with the language overtook mine around age three, so it was mostly evenings and weekdays I spent alone with her—something we were both glad of, given my temper, I think.

I'd take Hana to school, her always moaning about how long the walk was—about three hundred yards—and commenting on how the autumn "made the poor trees all naked." On one such November day, we brought a stick home, in from the cold, where it was immediately forgotten. Should a stick be for life or is it just for winter? At school, I'd chat with the other parents—every day stuff, apart from when Hana's daddy's friends were done for possession of amphetamines.

In the evenings, Hana would insist I play videogames for her pleasure, which was my idea of great parenting. On some weekends, I'd squash her between friends, and we'd drive to a race, the influence of which soon filtered through—my evil plan coming to fruition—as she clamoured to be allowed to compete also, only with the proviso that she should ride a pink bike, wear a dress and sandals, and have Barney, the sickeningly twee purple dinosaur, stuffed into a basket on the front. The bike snob still wrestles with the proud, supportive father on that issue.

Normality. It wasn't that bad.

It was a good year for Gail's lustre. She'd been nominated for and won the record industry's Woman of the Year Award, despite our rather image-damaging performance in '97. My girlfriend was in the country—our Cold War period on the wane, the Bulldozer of Love reducing the Berlin Wall around her heart to rubble—and we both dressed up for another swish night at a Mayfair hotel.

Compared with the last event, Gail's acceptance speech contained disappointingly few obscenities, but the location had hardly changed, and the scene was much the same: industry types, musicians of all degrees of fame, and all the free booze you could drink. That proved to be quite a lot in my case. Always a happy drunk, I exchanged half-cut pleasantries with Andy Ross, which was about all the conversation either of us could muster in that condition.

The band, bar the US bass-playing contingent, were there, invited to this as well as the previous event. It was a gesture not lost on me for much of the evening and during the taxi journey home as I contemplated the good fortune of having a manager who stood by us so staunchly. That had become pretty cherishable in the last three months.

food

Part of the deal my girlfriend struck with me in coming over was I had to make a Thanksgiving dinner. Silencing my objection to the importation of this outlandish foul feasting (two in the space of a month! Surely, no better evidence exists of a nation lost to decadence and moral despond—never mind the eleven-year-olds with guns …) I discovered shops in London that could service the demands of this festivity.

The party at my flat featured a host of friends including Gen and most of the band, A—part of a growing number of people we'd seen migrate from audience to backstage to our homes and then deservedly on to stages themselves. They were glumly convinced they'd just been dropped from London Records (they turned out to be wrong), and Gen was in similar circumstances. We laughed at the fact it was a loser's party. No-one with a record deal would be allowed in.

Two months later, we could invite the same people and have a winners party. Such is the weird world of the music industry.

15.

DECEMBER

Cherry, Bite 2

Here's a cliché I have particular pleasure to repeat for you. Publishing is where the money is in music. Every so often— supposedly once a year, until my deadline dodging wrecked that—EMI Music Publishing would give me a large sum of money, thereby commissioning me to write a set number of songs for them.

It often surprises people outside the industry that the hits I wrote aren't mine. They belong to the publishers who paid me an advance—an interest-free loan, essentially—and then a percentage of the royalties once they had accrued to a sum in excess of that loan. Somewhat confusingly, it's only the actual recordings of those songs that belong to the record company. But I digress.

My Christmas bonus came, and it was time to re-negotiate my publishing contract. Record sales had dwindled, and the band no longer had a deal, but DJs still spun our singles on the radio worldwide, other artists covered our songs, and advertisers used our hits as the soundtrack for enough commercials that I would soon be recouped on the advances from EMI Publishing, a fair incentive for them to want to re-sign me. Inevitably, it would be at a lower level than before, but once again, it was one of the better outcomes I had foreseen at the start of the year. If cycle couriering still loomed as a viable alternative, I could now choose the appropriate vehicle from a growing fleet of bikes.

Gail, Peter, Sally, and I met at the auspicious Ivy restaurant for lunch. Gail's bargaining approach was for me to shut up long enough for her to haggle before I undermined her with my sense of injustice at the figures involved for simply writing songs. Since food would be around at the time, this was no hardship for me. The subject wasn't even broached until dessert.

In two mouthfuls of something peachy, we discussed and agreed upon the general outline. I took another bite. Peter suggested a figure; Gail suggested another; they agreed to settle halfway; and I swallowed, having just earned enough to remain a top-rate income tax payer for some while longer. That and the peach made for a great, fleeting moment.

The speed of that decision making still amazes me.

3D Bass

So, I'd be writing again. But then, I'd never really stopped. Maybe I wasn't putting ideas into the computer or strumming chords on the guitar, but very little music passed my ears without careful analysis of chord sequences, lyrics, beats, bass lines, guitar effects, singing styles, influences, and, first and foremost, whether it amounted to one, great, cathartic surge or not. An overall impression formed in my mind, scraps of ideas constantly going into an electronic notepad, not as hectically as in previous years but now with more of a sense of enthralment than duty.

I went clubbing frequently again—drum 'n' bass nights, Metalheadz or Movement, sound systems where the bass carried the rock 'n' roll ethic through to the end of the millennium, huge slabs of low frequency that morphed from the speakers into a three-dimensional presence on the dance floor, an exhilarating and awe-inspiring force that made your scalp tingle and your bones vibrate. You felt it in the small of the back, in the solar plexus, and most firmly, in the soul—music that should have played in the cantina in *Star Wars*, a sound so ahead of its time and out of place that, even in modern London, conspiracy theories and dodgy photos can be discarded; alien life is audibly with us. That earthquake-bass allied with the rock-steady drums. An intriguingly weird and surprisingly fresh amalgamation of '60's rock patterns and 80's sounds is rock 'n' roll at this point in its genealogy.

Just as it was obvious the dance revolution of '88 would revolutionise popular music, just as it was clear in '92 The Prodigy would become one of the most exciting and influential bands of the decade, it's apparent drum 'n' bass will be the best thing to happen to rock in over ten years. It will probably happen as the music press champions a new group with the crippling influences of a couple of bands from 1985.

I contemplated this as I signed the new contract.

How Long?

I have one more bike reference. I couldn't find a race for December, the first month that year without at least one. Instead, I organised one, adding to the idea of being a freelance whatever-I-want-to-be by designing a course for a twenty-four-hour team race. Which, of course, I'd partake—two cold days in Staffordshire, riding my bike for hours on end and being well paid for it (courier practise?). My, but things were improving.

And in New York, things improved. I flew there for Christmas and discovered the perfect remedy for my flying phobia—10cl of neat vodka taken immediately before boarding. You may think that after seven years of international travel I was a little late coming to that antidote, but my earlier experiments with preflight alcohol had tended towards beer and miserable failure. Being dehydrated, bloated, and queasy doesn't ease the nerves, I found.

This scientific breakthrough impressed me so much that I continued the experiment throughout the flight, discovering *GI Jane* can be considered an acceptable film in certain circumstances and the dehydrated, bloated, and queasy feeling lurks with the patience inevitability lends it. Despite the hangover, I passed muster at immigration. It might not have been the first time my uniformed guardian of America's borders had encountered a red-eyed, hungover Brit in the line of duty.

I arrived in Manhattan, lay prone on a couch for two hours, and later fell asleep for fourteen—the best night's sleep I'd get all winter.

MTV's Christmas season featured their Top 250 videos of all time. "Right Here, Right Now" was at #187—not bad for a song I'd written almost exactly eight years before. I mean, I thought we were lucky to even be in there, luckier than most bands will ever be.

full Circle

Christmas flitted by, and my girlfriend's siblings had rented a house near the Catskill Mountains in upstate New York so we could all go snowboarding. The build up to New Year's Eve in a snowbound country house was very different from the year before in Brooklyn. No fireworks, no dutiful sense of occasion, less burning flesh. The Old Year got a good twenty-five-minute getaway before anyone had noticed the switch.

During the night, I had a vivid and unusually memorable dream. For an unexplained reason, I was a soldier, either in training or on active duty. I was part of a group of people acting individually but aiming to meet at an arranged rendezvous. For another unexplained reason, I had with me a pig I knew I would be using for food. Holed up for the evening in a hide, I skinned it in preparation for its imminent destruction. At some point, I became aware the pig had transformed into a representation of my daughter. Far from being in any obvious pain, the pig—now assuming the ability to speak with my own daughter's characteristics—was raring to go, urging me on in my mission, unquestioningly keen and blindly devoted to help me in any way she could. I couldn't tell if she understood the success of the operation she wanted to aid so eagerly relied on her demise. She was so guileless, so vulnerable, and so trusting—her innocent enthusiasm stark in the face of my careless, single-minded destruction, my selfish pursuit of "the mission" that to be aware of the scenario's probable outcome was utterly heartbreaking. In the dream, my body was wracked with sobbing so hard that later I found it hard to believe the tears didn't break through to the real world.

The next day, I realised the pig could also be representative of Gen, Iain, Alan, and Jerry—the rest of the band, the people who had always stood so fast behind me as I tried to lead us with equally unyielding stubbornness on our own particular mission. In the dream, something fundamental existed for me, something that goes direct and laser-guided to the soul, a smart bomb aimed at the psyche.

Throughout the first day of the New Year, thoughts troubled me that my cynicism, my bitterness, my obsessive tunnel vision will shape and change my daughter's life against her will, that she won't have the room or the chance to explore on her own, to live a life as I have done, to achieve something from the ordinary by virtue of encouragement, free will, and the joy of creativity. But I should give her more credit than that.

16.

JANUARY THE 1ST, 1998

Should Auld Lyrics be Forgot

During the drive to Hunter Mountain Ski Resort, "Right Here, Right Now" played on the radio. While I made my uncertain way down the mountain, the resort DJ further disturbed my concentration by also broadcasting the song, blasting it up the mountain from the ski centre along with the four songs US radio currently played to death.

Seven years after "Right Here, Right Now" had first broke through in America, I stood in enormous queues of people, waiting for the chance to purchase a lift ticket, rent snowboard boots and a board, and finally ride the lifts to the top of the slope. And while the song that had escalated me to a noticeable degree of worldwide fame played, no-one looked twice at me, no-one shouted *"OhmyGaaad!"* with that one and a half octave drop the name of the Lord gets in America, no wide-eyed women stopped me for an autograph, no-one called me an "asshole" while trying to focus an automatic camera. No-one even asked me how we got the name Jesus Jones.

On the flight home, people won't point at me and gesture to their friends in the queue for the airline check-in desk. When I sit on the plane, no-one will demand—not *request*—an autograph on a torn till receipt followed by another from the first person's friend then another from the kid they're sitting next to who wants to know what they're doing then one from the granny across the aisle who has no idea who I am but feels sure her granddaughter will and so on and so on until the air hostess intervenes on my behalf and gets me to do one final batch of forty autographs in one go instead.

Nope. I could ride the chairlift, swinging my half-frozen feet and just be that guy with the funny accent who always falls off the ski lift at the top—the incompetent snowboarder lying on his back, head down hill, the back of his trousers full of snow—and not the guy whose song gets played hundreds of times a year across the US, a song that gets wheeled out again every time some sort of minor public celebration occurs or just because a lot of people here thought it was a good tune and why not hear it again?

I liked it like that. But then, it was time to start writing again.

AFTERWARD

I had once again been in New York for long enough to not have to leave chalk marks along the streets of SoHo (and to know what that acronym means), to have discovered where best to go bike riding within the five boroughs of New York City (and to realise they're "boros" here), where to buy the best coffee, and to expect to go "postal" with an easily acquired automatic weapon the next time the regular series of untended car alarms goes off at 4 a.m.

Already got its US release a couple weeks later, and the promotion had been well underway. I had just returned from a week in Los Angeles, my first time to that previously triumphal conquest in five years. It hadn't changed at all, but it seemed like a new city from the way I had remember it when the band has made our first trip there at the start of the decade—wide-eyed at the opulence, the upliftingly blue sky, the maddeningly endless freeways forever jammed, the palm trees, and the lack of a TV set frame around every already familiar vista.

After the year you've just read about, it was hard to come to grips with the enthusiasm and open-mindedness I'd met on this familiar handshaking trail. Within five days, the press and radio schedule in America had eclipsed the number and quality of interviews we had done at home. Morning commuters across the country were listening to "The Next Big Thing," and the answer to the most popular question (after "Where have you been?") was that we'd tour in a couple of months' time. Dear God, I couldn't imagine what we would sound like in rehearsal after all that time.

Okay, so we weren't in the charts again, not on the front of *Rolling Stone*, not in the MTV clip people were sick of viewing, and opposition had come from the inevitable doubters in high places, but the same sense of hopelessness that would return to me when I had reread these pages didn't surface. It's no wonder British ex-rock stars pack the bars of Los Angeles, playing tiny solo gigs in the sunny suburbs.

Whatever the long-term legacy of *Already* will be, I had hoped for it to receive some recognition as a set of good songs by a good band. I had hoped for it to repay the rest of the band for the time they lost during the album's creation. I had hoped for it to repay some of the faith the people who had worked with us on the album had put in it. I had hoped for it to be a vindication for all the band's fans who had written in via the internet, the people who'd never know how gratifying their appreciation had been until they found themselves in the same situation as I had, the people who had bought the records and videos, who had come to the shows, and who had funded this adolescent dreamworld of mine.

Now, if you'll excuse me, I have a phoner to do.

"Well, we got the name …"

Acknowledgement

This tale is only possible because of the friendship of an almost random group of young men who came together and shared lows, highs, more lows, and recently more highs—my fellow bandsmen: Gen, Jerry, Alan, and Iain, with more than a tip of the hat to Tony Arthy and Gary Thatcher. I'm still in contact and very, very fond of Andy Ross, Dave Balfe, Gail Colson, Mike Mena, and Ian Huffam—folks who saw and believed in Jesus Jones when there was evidently every reason not to. Of course, none of the above would have mattered an iota if people had not bought records and come to shows, so the last and greatest of thanks go to all those fans of the band—past, present, and future.

Mike Edwards
June 2019
Dartmoor
UK

Make sure you haven't missed a Jesus Jones release. True fans have *ALL* the albums!
www.JesusJones.com